60 SECONDS TO SHINE
Volume II

221 ONE-MINUTE
MONOLOGUES FOR WOMEN

60 SECONDS TO *Shine*

VOLUME 2

221 ONE-MINUTE MONOLOGUES FOR WOMEN

EDITED BY
JOHN CAPECCI AND
IRENE ZIEGLER ASTON

MONOLOGUE AUDITION SERIES

A Smith and Kraus Book

Published by Smith and Kraus, Inc.
177 Lyme Road, Hanover, NH 03755
www.SmithandKraus.com

First Edition: April 2006
10 9 8 7 6 5 4 3 2 1

Cover and text design by Julia Hill Gignoux
Manufactured in the United States of America

The Monologue Audition Series   ISSN 1067-134X

Cataloging-in-Publication Data
60 seconds to shine. Volume 2, 221 one-minute monologues for women / edited by John Capecci and Irene Ziegler Aston.-- 1st ed.
    p. cm. -- (Monologue audition series, ISSN 1067-134X)
  ISBN 1-57525-401-8
  1. Monologues. 2. Acting--Auditions. 3. Women--Drama. I. Title: Sixty seconds to shine. II. Title: 221 one-minute monologues for women. III. Title: Two hundred and twenty one one-minute monologues for women. IV. Title: Two hundred twenty one one-minute monologues for women. V. Capecci, John. VI. Aston, Irene Ziegler, 1955- VII. Series.

PN2080.A1226 2006
808.82'45089287--dc22

                                                                    2006042305

TABLE OF CONTENTS

CLASSICAL MONOLOGUES

CONTEMPORARY MONOLOGUES

INTRODUCTION

Upon learning of today's typical cattle-call audition process, Dustin Hoffman—who hasn't had to audition in a long, long time—once declared that if he had only a minute to make an impression, he'd take off his clothes. For those of us who would rather think inside the box, here are two hundred and twenty-one monologues, all one minute or under in performance length.

For those auditions or class assignments where brevity is crucial, you need a monologue that gets to the point. You need a defined character, strong emotional content, and a resonant ending. Just as important, you need a lot of monologues from which to choose. This book offers you that, and more.

In our continuing effort to offer you new sources of monologues, we've drawn from plays, novels, short stories, poems, original monologues, essays, comics, novellas, radio plays, film scripts, and personal narratives.

How to Use This Book. At the back of this volume, you'll find all 221 monologues indexed according to *age, tone,* and *voice,* to help identify those most suited to your needs:

> **Age** is noted exactly only when specified by the author. More often, we've indicated an age range (20s, 20s-30s). In some instances, we've used a plus sign to show the character could be older than indicated, as in 40+.
>
> **Classic/Contemporary** refers to when the monologue was written, not necessarily when the character is speaking.

"Classic" texts are those that were written prior to the early 1920s.

Voice refers to indications of class, geography, ethnicity, nationality, sexual identity, or physicality that may help performers gain entry into an individual character, or closely "match" themselves to a monologue. The language of any text will reveal a certain level of education, class, or knowledge. Sometimes, however, a monologue arises out of specific cultural experience, demonstrated either through content or language. Those are the selections you'll find listed in the "Voice" index.

Whenever possible, we've attempted to excerpt monologues with a minimum of editing. Where editing was necessary, omissions are indicated by parenthetical ellipses (. . .). All other ellipses were part of the original text.

We offer appropriately brief contexts to help you gain some entry into the monologues. But, of course, in order to fully understand and ultimately embody the characters, you are strongly advised to read the play, novel, poem, etc. from which the monologue was drawn. The greater context must be fully explored in order to answer the all-important questions: who, what, when, where, why.

So—go forth and be brief. Just keep your shirt on.

ACKNOWLEDGMENTS

The editors are grateful to a number of people for assistance with these one-minute monologue books as well as the two-minute monologue books, in which we shamefully forgot to say thanks. Here then, is a double dose of appreciation to those who deserve much more:

Marisa Smith, Eric Kraus, and their staff, for taking us on.

The Department of Theatre and Dance, the University of Richmond, for the generous use of its excellent drama library.

D. L. Lepidus, for persisting in a thankless job.

Laurie Walker, for contributions and support.

All our smart and funny friends, who pointed us to their favorite monologues.

Graham and Rob, who get us.

Google™, which has changed our lives.

ACKNOWLEDGMENTS

CLASSICAL
MONOLOGUES

As You Like It

William Shakespeare

Play
20s-30s
Comic
Classical

*Dressed as a man, Rosalind guides her female suitor toward the
young shepherd who loves her.*

You foolish shepherd, wherefore do you follow her,
Like foggy south puffing with wind and rain?
You are a thousand times a properer man
Than she a woman: 'tis such fools as you
That makes the world full of ill-favour'd children:
'Tis not her glass, but you, that flatters her;
And out of you she sees herself more proper
Than any of her lineaments can show her.
But mistress, know yourself: down on your knees,
And thank heaven, fasting, for a good man's love:
For I must tell you friendly in your ear,
Sell when you can: you are not for all markets:
Cry the man mercy; love him; take his offer:
Foul is most foul, being foul to be a scoffer.
So take her to thee, shepherd: fare you well. (. . .)
Come, sister. Shepherdess, look on him better,
And be not proud: though all the world could see,
None could be so abused in sight as he.
Come, to our flock.

The Beaux' Strategem

George Farquhar

Play
40+
Comic
Classical

Mrs. Sullen warns her sister-in-law of the pitfalls of marriage.

O Sister, Sister! if ever you marry, beware of a sullen, silent Sot,
one that's always musing, but never thinks:—There's some
Diversion in a talking Blockhead; and since a woman must
wear Chains, I would have the Pleasure of hearing 'em rattle a
little.—Now you shall see, but take this by the way—He came
home this Morning at his usual Hour of Four, waken'd me out
of a sweet Dream of something else, by tumbling over the Tea-
table, which he broke all to pieces, after his Man and he had
rowl'd about the Room like sick Passengers in a Storm, he
comes flounce into Bed, dead as a Salmon into a Fishmonger's
Basket; his Feet cold as Ice, his Breath hot as a Furnace, and his
Hands and his Face as greasy as his Flannel Night-cap.—Oh
Matrimony!—He tosses up the Clothes with a barbarous swing
over his Shoulders, disorders the whole economy of my Bed,
leaves me half naked, and my whole Night's Comfort is the
tuneable Serenade of that wakeful Nightingale, his Nose.—O
the Pleasure of counting the melancholy Clock by a snoring
Husband!

The Clandestine Marriage

George Coleman and David Garrick

Play
18-20
Seriocomic
Classical

*Miss Sterling has managed to snag a fiancé above her station,
and she won't let her sister forget it.*

Never do I desire it—never, my dear Fanny, I promise you—Oh,
how I long to be transported to the dear regions of Grosvenor
Square—far—far from the dull districts of Aldersgate, Cheap,
Candlewick, and Farringdon Without and Within!—My heart
goes pit-a-pat at the very idea of being introduced at Court!—
gilt chariot!—piebald horses!—laced liveries!—and then the
whispers buzzing around the circle: "Who is that young lady?
Who is she?" "Lady Melvil, ma'am!" Lady Melvil! My ears tin-
gle at the sound—And then at dinner, instead of my father per-
petually asking: "Any news upon 'Change!" to cry: "Well, Sir
John! Anything new from Arthur's?"—or to say to some other
woman of quality: "Was your ladyship at the Duchess of
Rubber's last night?—Did you call in at Lady Thunder's? In the
immensity of crowd I swear I did not see you—Scarce a soul at
the opera last Saturday—Shall I see you at Carlisle House next
Thursday?"—Oh, the dear beau-monde! I was born to move in
the sphere of the great world.

The Comedy of Errors
William Shakespeare

Play
25+
Comic
Classical

Adriana believes that her husband is mad. Here, she makes her case to the Duke.

May it please your grace, Antipholus, my husband,
Whom I made lord of me and all I had,
At your important letters,—this ill day
A most outrageous fit of madness took him;
That desperately he hurried through the street,
With him his bondman, all as mad as he—
Doing displeasure to the citizens
By rushing in their houses, bearing thence
Rings, jewels, any thing his rage did like.
Once did I get him bound and sent him home,
Whilst to take order for the wrongs I went,
That here and there his fury had committed.
Anon, I wot not by what strong escape,
He broke from those that had the guard of him;
And with his mad attendant and himself,
Each one with ireful passion, with drawn swords,
Met us again and madly bent on us,
Chased us away; till, raising of more aid,
We came again to bind them. Then they fled
Into this abbey, whither we pursued them:
And here the abbess shuts the gates on us

And will not suffer us to fetch him out,
Nor send him forth that we may bear him hence.
Therefore, most gracious duke, with thy command
Let him be brought forth and borne hence for help.

The Constant Couple

George Farquhar

Play
20s-30s
Dramatic
Classical

Angelica beseeches Sir Harry to take inspiration from her own goodness and mind his manners.

What madness, Sir Harry, what wild dream of loose desire could prompt you to attempt this baseness? View me well. The brightness of my mind, methinks, should lighten outwards, and let you see your mistake in my behavior. I think it shines with so much innocence in my face, that it should dazzle all your vicious thoughts. Think now I am defenseless, 'cause alone. Your very self is guard against yourself: I'm sure, there's something generous in your soul; my words shall search it out, and eyes shall fire it for my own defense. Behold me, sire; view me with a sober thought, free from those fumes of wine that throw a mist before your sight, and you shall find that every glance from my reproaching eyes is arm'd with sharp resentment, and with a virtuous pride that looks dishonor dead.

Danton's Death
Georg Büchner
Translated by Henry J. Schmidt

Play
40s
Dramatic
Classical

In nineteenth-century France. Camille spews disrespect for the
masses who can only appreciate popular culture.

I tell you, if they aren't given everything in wooden copies, scat-
tered about in theaters, concerts, and art exhibits, they'll have
neither eyes nor ears for it. Let someone whittle a marionette
where the strings pulling it are plainly visible and whose joints
crack at every step in iambic pentameter: what a character,
what consistency! Let someone take a little bit of feeling, an
aphorism, a concept, and clothe it in a coat and pants, give it
hands and feet, color its face and let the thing torment itself
through three acts until it finally marries or shoots itself: an
idea! Let someone fiddle an opera which reflects the rising and
sinking of the human spirit the way a clay pipe with water imitates a nightingale: oh, art!

Take people out of the theater and put them in the street: oh,
miserable reality! (. . .) They see and hear nothing of Creation,
which renews itself every moment in and around them, glow-
ing, rushing, luminous. (. . .) The Greeks knew what they
were saying when they declared that Pygmalion's statue did
indeed come to life but never had any children.

The Double Inconstancy

By Marivaux
Translated and adapted by Stephen Wadsworth

Play
18-20
Dramatic
Classical

Silvia has been brought to the palace by the Prince who wishes to woo her, but she is in love with Harlequin, and she tells the servants she wants nothing to do with this scheme.

Very well, *my servant*, you think so highly of the honor shown me here—what do I need idle ladies-in-waiting spying on me for? They take away my lover and replace him with *women*? Hardly adequate compensation! And what do I care about all the singing and dancing they force me to sit through? A village girl happy in a little town is worth more than a princess weeping in a gorgeous suite of rooms. If the prince is so young and beautiful and full of desire, it's not my fault. He should keep all that for his equals and leave me to my poor Harlequin, who is no more a man of means than I am a woman of leisure, who is not richer than I am or fancier than I am, and who doesn't live in a bigger house than I do, but who *loves* me, without guile or pretense, and whom I love in return in the same way, and for whom I will die of a broken heart if I don't see him again soon. And what have they done to *him*? Perhaps they are mistreating him . . . *(SILVIA'S rage peaks.)* I am so angry! This is so unfair!

Emily Climbs

L. M. Montgomery

Novel
30s+
Seriocomic
Classical

Miss Janet Royal is the editor of a woman's magazine in New York, circa 1925. Here she attempts to convince the young Emily to move from the country to New York, where she can blossom as a writer.

Of course, I don't think you're ungrateful, (. . .) but I do—yes, I do think you are awfully foolish. You are simply throwing away your chances of a career. What can you ever do here that is worthwhile, child? You've no idea of the difficulties in your path. You can't get material here—there's no atmosphere—no—(. . .) no inspiration—you'll be hampered in every way—the big editors won't look farther than the address of P. E. Island on your manuscript. Emily, you're committing literary suicide. You'll realize that at three of the clock some white night, Emily B. (. . .) You'll get so tired of Blair Water—you'll know all the people in it—what they are and can be—it'll be like reading a book for the twentieth time. Oh, I know all about it. "I was alive before you were borned," as I said when I was eight, to a playmate of six. You'll get discouraged—the hour of three o'clock will gradually overwhelm you—there's a three o'clock every night, remember—you'll give up—(. . .)

Oh, I can see your whole life, Emily, here in a place like this where people can't see a mile beyond their nose.

Enemies
Maxim Gorky

Play
35+
Dramatic
Classical

The actress, Tatiana, talks of her creative frustration and despair.

I did once think that on the stage my feet were planted in solid ground . . . That I might grow tall . . . *(Emphatically, with distress.)* But now it's all so painful—I feel uncomfortable up there in front of those people, with their cold eyes saying, "Oh, we know all that, it's old, it's boring!" I feel weak and defenseless in front of them, I can't capture them, I can't excite them . . . I long to tremble in front of them with fear, with joy, to speak words full of fire and passion and anger, words that cut like knives, that burn like torches . . . I want to throw armfuls of words, throw them bounteously, abundantly, terrifyingly . . . So that people are set alight by them and shout aloud, and turn to flee from them . . . And then I'll stop them. Toss them different words. Words beautiful as flowers. Words full of hope and joy, and love. And they'll all be weeping, and I'll weep too . . . wonderful tears. They applaud. Smother me with flowers. Bear me up on their shoulders. For a moment—I hold sway over them all . . . Life is there, in that one moment, all of life, in a single moment. Everything that's best is always in a single moment.

Hamlet
William Shakespeare

Play
30+
Dramatic
Classical

Queen Gertrude recounts Ophelia's death to Laertes, Ophelia's brother.

One woe doth tread upon another's heel,
So fast they follow: your sister's drown'd, Laertes. (. . .)
There is a willow grows aslant a brook,
That shows his hoar leaves in the glassy stream;
There with fantastic garlands did she come
Of crow-flowers, nettles, daisies, and long purples
That liberal shepherds give a grosser name,
But our cold maids do dead men's fingers call them:
There, on the pendant boughs her coronet weeds
Clambering to hang, an envious sliver broke;
When down her weedy trophies and herself
Fell in the weeping brook. Her clothes spread wide;
And, mermaid-like, awhile they bore her up:
Which time she changed snatches of old tunes;
As one incapable of her own distress,
Or like a creature native and indued
Unto that element: but long it could not be
Till that her garments, heavy with their drink,
Pull'd the poor wretch from her melodious lay
To muddy death. (. . .)
Drown'd, drown'd.

Ivanov

Anton Chekhov
Translation by Mason W. Cartwright

Play
30+
Dramatic
Classical

Anna Petrovna loves her husband, though he treats her poorly. Ill, she speaks to her doctor.

I am beginning to think that fate has cheated me, Doctor. (. . .)

. . . My dear friend, you are always so considerate of me, so tactful, you are afraid to tell me the truth, but do you think I don't know what my illness is? I know perfectly well . . .

Can you tell funny stories? Nikolai can. You say that Nikolai is this or that, one thing and another. How can you know him? Is it possible to know a man in six months? That is a remarkable man, Doctor, and I am sorry you didn't know him two or three years ago. Now he's depressed, he doesn't talk, he doesn't do anything, but then . . . how fascinating he was! I fell in love with him at first sight. I just looked at him and the trap was sprung! He said, "Come," and I cut myself off from everything; it was just like cutting dead leaves with a scissors, and I went . . . But now, it's different . . . Now he goes to the Lebedevs' to amuse himself with other women, and I . . . I sit in the garden and listen to owls screech.

A Journey to London
Sir John Vanbrugh

Play
20s-30s
Comic
Classical

Lady Arabella assures her young friend that marriage does not kill scintillating conversation.

Clarinda, you are the most mistaken in the world; marry'd People have things to talk of, Child, that never enter into the Imagination of others. (. . .) Oh, there's no Life like it. This very Day now for Example, my Lord and I, after a pretty cheerful *tête à tête* Dinner, sat down by the Fire-side, in an idle, indolent, pick-tooth Way for a while, as if we had not thought of another's being in the Room. At last (stretching himself, and yawning twice) My Dear, says he, you came home very late last Night. 'Twas but Two in the Morning, says I. I was in bed (yawning) by Eleven, says he. So you are every Night, says I. Well, says he, I am amazed, how you can sit up so late. How can you be amazed, says I, at a Thing that happens so often. Upon which, we enter'd into Conversation. And tho', this is a Point has entertain'd us above fifty times already, we always find so many pretty new Things to say upon't that I believe in my Soul it will last as long as we live.

Julius Caesar

William Shakespeare

Play
30+
Dramatic
Classical

*Plagued with guilt over his imminent betrayal of Caesar, Brutus
leaves his bed to roam. Portia, having endured her husband's
behavior as along as she can, begs him to tell what's going on.*

Brutus, my lord! (. . .) You've ungently, Brutus,
Stole from my bed: and yesternight, at supper,
You suddenly arose, and walk'd about,
Musing and sighing, with your arms across,
And when I ask'd you what the matter was,
You stared upon me with ungentle looks;
I urged you further; then you scratch'd your head,
And too impatiently stamp'd with your foot;
Yet I insisted, yet you answer'd not,
But, with an angry wafture of your hand,
Gave sign for me to leave you: so I did;
Fearing to strengthen that impatience
Which seem'd too much enkindled and withal
Hoping it was but an effect of humour,
Which sometime hath his hour with every man. (. . .)
Within the bond of marriage, tell me, Brutus,
Is it expected I should know no secrets
That appertain to you? Am I yourself
But, as it were, in sort of limitation,
To keep you at meals, comfort your bed,
And talk to you sometimes? Dwell I but in the suburbs
Of your good pleasure? If it be no more,
Portia is Brutus' harlot, not his wife.

King Henry IV, Part 1

William Shakespeare

Play
20s-30s
Dramatic
Classical

Lady Percy entreats her troubled warrior husband, Hotspur, to confide in her.

O, my good lord, why are you thus alone?
For what offence have I this fortnight been
A banish'd woman from my Harry's bed?
Tell me, sweet lord, what ist that takes from thee
Thy stomach, pleasure and thy golden sleep? (. . .)
In thy faint slumbers I by thee have watch'd,
And heard thee murmur tales of iron wars;
Speak terms of manage to thy bounding steed;
Cry 'Courage! To the field!' (. . .)
Thy spirit within thee hath been so at war
And thus hath so bestirr'd thee in thy sleep,
That beads of sweat have stood upon thy brow,
Like bubbles in a late-disturbed stream;
And in thy face strange motions have appear'd,
Such as we see when men strain their breath
On some great sudden hest. O, what portents are these?
Some heavy business hath my lord in hand,
And I must know, else he loves me not.

King John
William Shakespeare

Play
30s-50s
Dramatic
Classical

Constance has been driven crazy with grief. Her son, Arthur has been captured by King John of England, and will surely be put to death. Deserted, haggard, and demented, she confronts King Philip of France, the Dauphin Lewis, and Pandulph, then woos death as might a maid woo a husband.

No: I defy all counsel, all redress,
But that which ends all counsel, true redress,
Death, death; O amiable lovely death!
Thou odoriferous stench! sound rottenness!
Arise forth from the couch of lasting night,
Thou hate and terror to prosperity,
And I will kiss thy detestable bones
And put my eyeballs in thy vaulty brows
And ring these fingers with thy household worms
And stop this gap of breath with fulsome dust
And be a carrion monster like thyself:
Come, grin on me, and I will think thou smilest
And buss thee as thy wife. Misery's love,
O, come to me.

King John
William Shakespeare

Play
30s-50s
Dramatic
Classical

Constance has been driven crazy with grief. Her son, Arthur has been captured by King John of England, and will surely be put to death. Deserted, haggard, and demented, she confronts King Philip of France, the Dauphin Lewis, and Pandulph.

And, father cardinal, I have heard you say
That we shall see and know our friends in heaven;
If that be true, I shall see my boy again;
For since the birth of Cain, the first male child,
To him that did but yesterday suspire,
There was not such a gracious creature born.
But now will canker sorrow eat my bud
And chase the native beauty from his cheek
And he will look as hollow as a ghost
As dim and meagre as an ague's fit,
And so he'll die; and rising so again,
When I shall meet him the court of heaven
I shall not know him; therefore never, never
Must I behold my pretty Arthur more. (. . .)

Grief fills the room up of my absent child,
Lies in his bed, walks up and down with me,
Puts on his pretty looks, repeats his words,
Remembers me of all his gracious parts,

Stuffs out his vacant garments with his form;
Then, have I reason to be fond of grief?
Fare you well: had you such a loss as I,
I could give better comfort than you do.

King Lear
William Shakespeare

Play
30s
Dramatic
Classical

Goneral is tired of her aging father's behaviors. She speaks to her steward, Oswald.

By day and night he wrongs me; every hour
He flashes into one gross crime or other,
That sets us all at odds: I'll not endure it:
His knights grow riotous, and himself upbraids us
On every trifle. When he returns from hunting,
I will not speak with him; say I am sick:
If you come slack of former services,
You shall do well; the fault of it I'll answer. (. . .)

Put on what weary negligence you please,
You and your fellows; I'll have it come to question:
If he dislike it, let him to our sister,
Whose mind and mine, I know, in that are one,
Not to be over-ruled. Idle old man,
That still would manage those authorities
That he hath given away! Now, by my life,
Old fools are babes again; and must be used
With cheques as flatteries,—when they are seen abused.
Remember what I tell you.

King Richard III

William Shakespeare

Play
20s-30s
Dramatic
Classical

Lady Anne halts the funeral bier to grieve for King Henry VI, murdered in cold blood with the participation of Richard, also responsible for the murder of Anne's husband. Richard desires Anne for her blue blood and political assets. She despises and curses him.

Set down, set down your honourable load,
If honour may be shrouded in a hearse,
Whilst I awhile obsequiously lament
The untimely fall of virtuous Lancaster.
Poor key-cold figure of a holy king!
Pale ashes of the house of Lancaster!
Thou bloodless remnant of that royal blood!
Be it lawful that I invocate thy ghost,
To hear the lamentations of poor Anne,
Wife to thy Edward, to thy slaughter'd son,
Stabb'd by the selfsame hand that made these wounds!
Lo, in thee windows that let forth thy life
I pour the helpless balm of my poor eyes.
Cursed be the hand that made these fatal holes!
Cursed be the heart that had the heart to do it!
Cursed the blood that let this blood from hence!

King Richard III
William Shakespeare

Play
20s-30s
Dramatic
Classical

*Lady Anne halts the funeral bier of King Henry VI to curse
Richard for the deaths of the king and her husband, murdered
in cold blood.*

Cursed be the hand that made these fatal holes!
Cursed be the heart that had the heart to do it!
Cursed the blood that let this blood from hence!
More direful hap betide that hated wretch,
That makes us wretched by the death of thee,
Than I can wish to adders, spiders, toads,
Or any creeping venom'd thing that lives!
If ever he have child, abortive be it,
Prodigious, and untimely brought to light,
Whose ugly and unnatural aspect
May fright the hopeful mother at the view;
And that be heir to his unhappiness!
If ever he have wife, let her be made
As miserable by the death of him
As I am made by my poor lord and thee!
Come, now toward Chertsey with your holy load,
Taken from Paul's to be interred there;
And still, as you are weary of the weight,
Rest you, whiles I lament King Henry's corse.

The Lanchashire Witches

Thomas Shadwell

Play
20+
Dramatic
Classical

Mrs. Dickenson, a witchy witch, describes a recent forage for special ingredients.

From the Seas slimy 'ouse a Weed
I fetch'd to open Locks at need.
With Coats tuck'd up and with my Hair,
All flowing loosely in the Air,
With naked Feet I went among
The poysonus Plants, there Adders Tongue,
With Aconite and Martagon,
Henbane, Hemlock, Moon-wort too,
Wild Fig-Tree, that o're Tombs do's grow,
The deadly Night-shade, Cypress, Yew,
And Libbards Bane, and venomous Dew,
I gathered for my Charms. Harg. And I
Dug up a Mandrake, which did cry.
Three Circles I made, and the Wind was good,
And looking to the West I stood.

Leves Amores

Katherine Mansfield

Short story
Late 20s–30s
Dramatic
Classical

*In the early 1900s, a woman fears youth has passed her by,
until her passions are restored.*

And I sat on the bed, and thought: "Come, this Old Age. I have
forgotten passion, I have been left behind in the beautiful gold-
en procession of Youth. (. . .)"

Was Youth dead?. . . *Was* Youth dead?

She told me as we walked along the corridor to her room that
she was glad the night had come. I did not ask why. I was glad,
too. It seemed a secret between us. So I went with her into her
room to undo those troublesome hooks. She lit a little candle
on an enamel bracket. The light filled the room with darkness.
Like a sleepy child she slipped out of her frock and then, suddenly, turned to me and flung her arms round my neck. Every
bird upon the bulging frieze broke into song. Every rose upon
the tattered paper budded and formed into blossom. Yes, even
the green vine upon the bed curtains wreathed itself into
strange chaplets and garlands, twined round us in a leafy
embrace. (. . .)

And Youth was not dead.

Little Women

Louisa May Alcott

Novel
15
Comic
Classical

Jo resists her transition to womanhood.

I hate affected, niminy-piminy chits! (. . .)

I'm not [a young lady]! and if turning up my hair makes me one, I'll wear it in two tails till I'm twenty! (. . .) I hate to think I've got to grow up, and be Miss March, and wear long gowns, and look as prim as a China-aster! It's bad enough to be a girl, anyway, when I like boys' games and work and manners! I can't get over my disappointment in not being a boy; and it's worse than ever now, for I'm dying to go and fight with papa, and I can only stay at home and knit, like a poky old woman!

Love in a Village
Isaac Bickerstaff

Play
40s
Seriocomic
Classical

Mrs. Woodstock, upon learning her niece plans to elope with her music teacher, foolishly tries to distract the girl with needlepoint.

This is mighty pretty romantic stuff! But you learn it out of your play-books and novels. Girls in my time had other employments; we worked at our needles, and kept ourselves from idle thoughts: before I was your age, I had finished, with my own fingers, a complete set of chairs, and a fire-screen in ten-stitch; four counterpanes in Marseilles quilting; and the Creed and Ten Commandments, in the hair of our family: it was fram'd and glaz'd, and hung over the parlour chimney piece, and your poor dear grandfather was prouder of it than e'er a picture in his house. I never looked into a book, but when I aid my prayers, except it was the Complete Housewife, or the great family receipt-book: whereas you are always at your studies! Ah, I never knew a woman come to good, that was fond of reading.

A Midsummer Night's Dream

William Shakespeare

Play
Late teens–early 20s
Dramatic
Classical

Puck's spell having gone awry, Helena is being pursued by two men who once spurned her, and she believes she is the object of a cruel joke. Worse, she believes her childhood friend, Hermia, has joined them in their ridicule.

Now I perceive you have conjoin'd all three
To fashion this false sport, in spite of me.
Injurious Hermia! most ungrateful maid!
Have you conspired, have you with thee contrived
To bait me with this foul derision?
Is all the counsel that we two have shared,
The sisters' vows, the hours that we have spent,
When we have chid the hasty-footed time
For parting us,—O, is it all forgot?
All school-days' friendship, childhood innocence?
We, Hermia, like two artificial gods,
Have with our needles created both one flower,
Both on one sampler, sitting on one cushion,
Both warbling of one song, both in one key,
As if our hands, our sides, voices and minds,
Had been incorporate. (. . .)
And will you rent our ancient love asunder,
To join with men in scorning your poor friend?
It is not friendly, 'tis not maidenly:
Our sex, as well as I, may chide you for it,
Though I alone do feel the injury.

A Midsummer Night's Dream
William Shakespeare

Play
Late teens-early 20s
Dramatic
Classical

Pucks's spell gone awry, Helena is being pursued by two men who once spurned her, and she believes she is the object of a cruel joke. Worse, she believes her childhood friend, Hermia, has joined them in their ridicule.

Have you not set Lysander, as in scorn,
To follow me and praise my eyes and face?
And made your other love, Demetrius,
Who even but now did spurn me with his foot,
To call me goddess, nymph, divine and rare,
Precious, celestial? Wherefore speaks he this
To her he hates? and wherefore doth Lysander
Deny your love, so rich within his soul,
And tender me, forsooth, affection,
But by your setting on, by your consent?
What though I be not so in grace as you,
So hung upon with love, so fortunate,
But miserable most, to love unloved?
This you should pity rather than despise. (. . .)
Ay, do, persever, counterfeit sad looks,
Make mouths upon me when I turn my back;
Wink at each other; hold the sweet jest up:
This sport, well carried, shall be chronicled.

If you have any pity, grace, or manners,
You would not make me such an argument.
But fare ye well: 'tis partly my own fault;
Which death or absence soon shall remedy.

A Midsummer Night's Dream
William Shakespeare

Play
30s+
Comic
Classical

Titania wakes from her sleep and, because of Oberon's spell, falls hopelessly in love with Bottom (upon whom Puck has fixed a donkey's head).

Out of this wood do not desire to go:
Thou shalt remain here, whether thou wilt or no.
I am a spirit of no common rate;
The summer still doth tend upon my state;
And I do love thee: therefore go with me.
I'll give thee fairies to attend on thee;
And they shall fetch thee jewels from the deep,
And sing, while thou on pressed flowers dost sleep:
Peaseblossom! Cobweb! Moth! and Mustardseed!
Be kind and courteous to this gentleman;
Feed him with apricocks and dewberries,
With purple grapes, green figs, and mulberries;
And pluck the wings from painted butterflies
To fan the moonbeams from his sleeping eyes.
Nod to him, elves, and do him courtesies.

A Midsummer Night's Dream
William Shakespeare

Play
20+
Comic
Classical

In this closing monologue, Puck suggests that the last two hours have been a dream.

If we shadows have offended,
Think but this, and all is mended,
That you have but slumber'd here
While these visions did appear.
And this weak and idle theme,
No more yielding but a dream,
Gentles, do not reprehend:
if you pardon, we will mend:
And, as I am an honest Puck,
If we have unearned luck
Now to 'scape the serpent's tongue,
We will make amends ere long;
Else the Puck a liar call;
So, good night unto you all.
Give me your hands, if we be friends,
And Robin shall restore amends.

The Misanthrope

Molière

Translated by Hal Gelb

Play
30s-40s
Comic
Classical

Arsinoe thinks she has a chance against Celimene in winning the love of Alceste (the misanthrope). Arsinoe is a spiteful woman, a loser at love who hides her failures under a mask of piety and propriety. Here, she puts Celimene down, while pretending to be a friend.

Yesterday, I was at the home of some of the most righteous
    people imaginable,
When suddenly the conversation
Turned to you. In that house, your behavior
Was unfortunately not looked on with favor.
The flirtations—and the conventions that they flout—
The crowd of men here who stream, shall we say, in and out,
Were, in fact, so severely faulted,
My breathing nearly halted.
Well, you can imagine whose side I took;
Why, I did everything I could defending you.
But there are things one can't excuse however much you'd like
    to,
And in the end I was forced to admit your way of life
Creates a bad impression and gives birth to shocking rumors.
Not that I believe your virtue has been compromised.
No, no, no, heaven forbid.

But the world maintains that where there's smoke, there are
    flames.
One must enact
The appearance of propriety as well as propriety in fact.
Fortunately, Madam, your soul is far too sensible I'm sure
To dismiss this profitable advice and attribute it
To motives other than my zealous desire for your welfare.

The Misanthrope

Molière

Translated by Hal Gelb

Play
Early 20s
Comic
Classical

Celimene barely hides her anger at a veiled attack by her competitor, Arsinoe. She attempts to hide it under the guise of returning profitable advice.

Madam, thank you a thousand times.
And just as you proved yourself a friend
By showing how I looked in other people's view,
I'll imitate your sweet example
And let you know what people have to say about you.
In a house where I was visiting the other day
Some men of very great virtue were discussing what matters
To a truly moral soul. And your name came up.
Strange to say though,
Your prudery, fanaticism and sisterly concern
Weren't cited as examples of behavior
Dear to the heart of our Blessed Savior.
What's the point, they asked, of her modest mien and pious
    exterior,
When what's inside is so inferior.
Yes, in devout circles, she makes a great display of fervor,
But home alone, she just hopes some man sometime somehow
    will have her.
That's what they said, Madam. As for me,

I defended you assiduously.
I assured them that what they were reciting
Was merely backbiting.
But their chorus of opinion
Unfortunately,
Triumphed over my lone voice in the wind.

Much Ado About Nothing

William Shakespeare

Play
Early 20s
Comic
Classical

Beatrice overhears Hero and Ursula talking about Benedick, and thinks he loves her.

What fire is in mine ears? Can this be true?
Stand I condemn'd for pride and scorn so much?
Contempt, farewell! and maiden pride, adieu!
No glory lives behind the back of such.
And, Benedick, love on; I will requite thee,
Taming my wild heart to thy loving hand:
If thou dost love, my kindness shall incite thee
To bind our loves up in a holy band;
For others say thou dost deserve, and I
Believe it better than reportingly.

Othello
William Shakespeare

Play
20s-30s
Dramatic
Classical

Desdemona, clueless as to why her husband has accused her of adultery, resigns.

O good Iago,
What shall I do to win my lord again?
Good friend, go to him; for, by this light of heaven,
I know not how I lost him. Here I kneel:
If e'er my will did trespass 'gainst his love,
Either in discourse of thought or actual deed,
Or that mine eyes, mine ears, or any sense,
Delighted them in any other form;
Or that I do not yet, and ever did.
And ever will—though he do shake me off
To beggarly divorcement—love him dearly,
Comfort forswear me! Unkindness may do much;
And his unkindness may defeat my life,
But never taint my love. I cannot say "whore:"
It does abhor me now I speak the word;
To do the act that might the addition earn
Not the world's mass of vanity could make me.

Pericles

William Shakespeare

Play
20+
Dramatic
Classical

Dionyza gives Leonine final encouragement on how to kill Marina, who appears conveniently, affording an immediate opportunity.

Thy oath remember; thou has sworn to do't:
'Tis but a blow, which never shall be known.
Thou canst not do thing in the world so soon,
To yield thee so much profit. Let no conscience,
Which is but cold, inflaming love I' thy bosom,
Inflame too nicely; nor let pity, which
Even women have cast off, melt thee, but be
A soldier to thy purpose. (. . .)
Here she comes weeping for her nurse's death. Thou art resolved?

How now, Marina! why do you keep alone? (. . .)
Come, give me your flowers, ere the sea mar it.
Walk with Leonine; the air is quick there,
And it pierces and sharpens the stomach. Come,
Leonine, take her by the arm, walk with her. (. . .)

Walk half an hour, Leonine, at the least:
Remember what I have said.

The Prince of Parthia

Thomas Godfrey

Play
40s
Dramatic
Classical

When the Queen discovers the King has fallen in love with a young beauty, she ignores her maid's protests (Edessa), and she levels a dark curse.

Soft is thy nature, but alas! Edessa,
Thy heart's a stranger to a mother's sorrows,
To see the pride of all her wishes blasted,
Thy fancy cannot paint the storm of grief,
Despair and anguish, which my breast has known.
Oh! shower, ye Gods, your torments on Arsaces,
Curs'd be the morn, which dawned upon his birth.

Away! for I will curse—
O may he never know father's fondness,
Or know it to his sorrow, may his hopes
Of joy be cut like mine, and his short life
Be one continu'd tempest: if he lives,
Let him be curs'd with jealousy and fear,
And vext with anguish of neglecting scorn;
May tort'ring hope present the flowing cup,
Then hasty snatch it from his eager thirst,
And when he dies base treach'ry be the means.

Yes, I'll now be calm,
Calm as the sea when the rude waves are laid,
And nothing but a gentle swell remains;
My curse is heard, and I shall have revenge.

The Rebellion

Thomas Rawlins

Play
20s-30s
Dramatic
Classical

Aurelia implores the powers that be to save Antonio.

Oft have I heard my brother with a tongue
Proud of the office praise this lovely lord;
And my trapped soul did with as eager haste
Draw in the breath; and now, o Aurelia!
Buried with him just all the joy thou hast
Forever sleep; and with a pale consumption,
Pitying him, wilt thou thyself be ruined?
He must not die; if there be any way
Reveal'd to the distressed, I will find it.
Assist a poor lost virgin, some good power,
And lead her to a path, whose secret tract
May guide both him and me unto our safety.
Be kind, good wits, I never until now
Put you to any trouble; 'tis your office
To help at need this little world you live by;
(She thinks.)
Not yet! O, dullness, do not make me mad—
I have't, blessed brains! Now shall a woman's wit
Wrestle with fate, and if my plot but hit,
Come off with wreaths. My duty, nay, may all,
I must forsake, lest my Antonio fall.

The Relapse

Sir John Vanbrugh

Play
20s-30s
Dramatic
Classical

Amanda discovers her lover's infidelity and vows revenge.

Would the world were on fire, and you in the middle on't.
Begone; leave me.
At last I am convinced. My eyes are testimonies
Of his falsehood. The base, ungrateful, perjured villain.
Good gods, what slippery stuff are men composed of?
Sure the account of their creation's false
And 'twas the woman's rib they were formed of. (. . .)
'Tis an ill cause, indeed, where nothing's to be said for't.
My beauty possibly is in the wane;
Perhaps sixteen has greater charms for him.
Yes, there's the secret. But let him know,
My quiver's not entirely emptied yet:
I still have darts and I can shoot 'em too,
They're not so blunt but they can enter still,
The want's not in my power, but in my will.
Virtue's his friend, or, through another's heart
I yet could find the way to make him smart.

A Room with a View

E. M. Forster

Novel
50s+
Comic
Classical

On an outing in the Italian countryside, the long-suffering Charlotte Lavish urges her charge, the young Lucy, to sit upon a canvas square on the ground. Charlotte will be perfectly fine sitting on the cold earth. . .

How tired one gets. (. . .) Oh, I do wish Freddy and your mother could be here.

Then you sit down. (*She produces a canvas square that she had the foresight to bring along.*) Observe my foresight.

(*LUCY urges CHARLOTTE to sit on the canvas. She declines.*)

(. . .) Without a moment's doubt, Lucy. The ground will do for me. Really I have not had rheumatism for years. If I do feel it coming on I shall stand. Imagine your mother's feelings if I let you sit in the wet in your white linen. (. . .) *(They sit.)* Here we are, all settled delightfully. Even if my dress is thinner it will not show so much, being brown. Sit down, dear; you are too unselfish; you don't assert yourself enough. (. . .) (*She coughs.*) Now don't be alarmed; this isn't a cold. It's the tiniest cough, and I have had it three days. It's nothing to do with sitting here at all.

The Rover
Alphra Behn

Play
20s-30s
Dramatic
Classical

Lucetta, a galley whore and slave, empathizes with an Essex calf aboard the ship.

This gold will buy us things. Alas, I curse my future that has made me a slave to Sancho, since I was sold. Would I had coin enough to fly to England and try my fortune as the colonel did. But what base means we girls o' the galleys must submit to, ere we can gain our ends. A common whore; oh fie; one that must yield to all beastly embraces, yea, all the nasty devices men's lust can invent; nay, not only obey but the fire, too, and hazard all diseases when their lust commands. And so sometimes we are enjoyed aforetimes, but never after. And yet I cannot but laugh at this English fool. If I cannot rise in this bad world, yet 'tis some recompense to bring such a fellow down. O, now is this bull calf as naked as I was once on shipboard, and now I pity him. There's for thee, poor Essex calf.

The Ruddigore or
The Witch's Curse
William Schwenk Gilbert

Play
18-20
Seriocomic
Classical

Rose tells her aunt that she has no suitors because she lives strictly by her book of etiquette, and she can find no suitor worthy.

Hush, dear aunt, for thy words pain me sorely. Hung in a plated dish-cover to the knocker of the work-house door, with naught that I could call mine own, save a change of baby-linen and a book of etiquette, little wonder if I have always regarded that work as a voice from a parent's tomb. This hallowed volume *(Producing a book of etiquette.)*, composed, if I may believe the title-page, by no less an authority than the wife of a Lord Mayor, has been, through life, my guide and monitor. By its solemn precepts I have learnt to test the moral worth of all who approach me. The man who bites his bread, or eats peas with a knife, I look upon as a lost creature, and he who has not acquired the proper way of entering and leaving a room is the object of my pitying horror. There are those in this village who bite their nails, dear aunt, and nearly all are wont to use their pocket combs in public places. In truth I could pursue this painful theme much further, but behold, I have said enough.

The Sack of Rome

Mercy Otis Warren

Play
20s-30s
Dramatic
Classical

*As Rome falls, Edoxia resigns herself and deplores the violent
nature of man.*

Where shall I fly? to what sequestered shade
Where the world's distant din no more alarms,
Or warring passions burst through nature's tie
And make mankind creation's a foulest stain.
Horror and guilt stare wild in every eye;
Freedom extinguished in the flames of lust
Bleeds fresh beside Rome's long expiring fame;
Virtue's become the rude barbarian's jest,
Bartered for gold, and floating down the tide
Of foreign vice, stained with domestic guilt!
Oh, could I hide in some dark hermitage
Beneath some hollow, dismal, broken cliff,
I'd weep forlorn the miseries of Rome
Till time's last hollow broke, and left me quiet
On the naked strange. Ah! Leo,
Durst thou be still the friend of sad Eudoxia?
Hast thou the courage yet to visit grief,
And sooth a wretch by sympathetic tears
And reconcile me to the name of man?
Canst show me one less cruel than the tiger
Nursed in the wilds and feasting on the flesh
Of all but his own species?
This predilection's left to man alone,
To drink and riot on his brother's blood.

The Sea Gull

Anton Chekhov
Translated by Mason W. Cartwright

Play
43
Dramatic
Classical

Arkadina's lover, the writer Trigorin, has admitted his fascination with Nina, a much younger actress. Arkadina reacts with all the fear, anger, and drama one would expect of a threatened actress.

Am I so old and ugly you can talk to me like this about other women? (*She embraces and kisses him.*) You've lost your mind! (*Falls to her knees.*) You're my happiness, my joy, my life! (*Hugging his knees.*) If you leave me, even for an hour, I won't make it, I'll lose my mind, my wonderful beautiful man. My master. (*Kisses his hands.*) You're everything to me, you crazy boy, everything! You think I'm going to let you go off and do something crazy? Never. (*Laughs.*) You're mine. Mine! (*Touches him.*) This forehead's mine, these eyes are mine. You're all mine! And you're so talented, gifted, the best of all our writers, Russia's only hope. You write with such sincerity and freshness and humor, you can bring to light the depths of people and places with a single stroke of the pen. Your characters live! It's impossible to read you without being uplifted. You think I'm exaggerating? Flattering? No never. You don't believe me? Just look in my eyes . . . Go ahead, look. Do you see a liar? I'm the only one who can truly appreciate you, who'll tell you the truth, my dear darling. You will come with me won't you? You're not going to leave me, are you?

The Sea Gull

Anton Chekhov

Translated by Mason W. Cartwright

Play
43
Seriocomic
Classical

Arkadina, still a beautiful actress at forty-three, exhibits vanity and egotism.

Stand up, stand next to me. (*They stand.*) There, now—look. You're only twenty-two, and I'm almost twice your age. Let me ask you, who looks younger? Me, of course. And you know why? Because I'm working, I'm involved, I'm on the move constantly, while you stay in one place day after day. You're not living. And another thing. I have this rule. I never dwell on the future. Never. Never think about dying. What will be, will be. And I'm very particular about myself, too. As particular as an English noblewoman. My dear, as the saying goes, I keep myself up. I'm always well-dressed and my hair well-styled. You think I'd leave the house, even come into the garden looking sloppy? Never. The reason I look so good for my age is because I've never let myself go as so many women do. (*Paces up and down the lawn with arms akimbo.*) There. See that? Light as a feather. I could play the part of fifteen-year-old girl, right now. Now, let's get on with the reading. It's my turn. Where were we?

Sonnet XVIII
William Shakespeare

Poem
20+
Dramatic
Classical

The speaker searches for the perfect analogy of her love's eternal beauty.

Shall I compare thee to a summer's day?
Thou art more lovely and more temperate:
Rough winds do shake the darling buds of May,
And summer's lease hath all too short a date:
Sometime too hot the eye of heaven shines,
And often is his gold complexion dimmed,
And every fair from fair sometime declines,
By chance, or nature's changing course untrimmed:
But thy eternal summer shall not fade,
Nor lose possession of that fair thou ow'st,
Nor shall death brag thou wander'st in his shade,
When in eternal lines to time thou grow'st,
 So long as men can breathe, or eyes can see,
 So long lives this, and this gives life to thee.

Sonnet XXX
William Shakespeare

Poem
40+
Dramatic
Classical

The speaker looks back on life and its sorrows.

When to the sessions of sweet, silent thought
I summon up remembrances of things past,
I sigh the lack of many a thing I sought,
And with old woes new wail my dear time's waste;
Then can I drown an eye (unused to flow)
For precious friends hid in death's dateless night,
And weep afresh love's long since cancelled woe,
And moan the expense of many a vanished sight.
Thus can I grieve at grievances foregone,
And heavily from woe to woe tell o'er
The sad account of fore bemoaned moan,
Which I new pay, as if not paid before;
   But if the while I think on thee, dear friend,
   All losses are restored, and sorrows end.

Sudden Light

Dante Gabriel Rossetti

Poem
20s-30s
Dramatic
Classical

Romantic déjà vu, and the endurance of love.

I have been here before,
But when or how I cannot tell:
I know the grass beyond the door,
The sweet keen smell,
The sighing sound, the lights around the shore.
You have been mine before,—
How long ago I may not know:
But just when at that swallow's soar
Your neck turn'd so,
Some veil did fall,—I knew it all of yore.
Has this been thus before?
And shall not thus time's eddying flight
Still with our lives our love restore
In death's despite,
And day and night yield one delight once more?

Titus Andronicus
William Shakespeare

Play
40+
Dramatic
Classical

Tamora pleads for her sons' lives.

Stay, Roman brethren! Gracious conqueror,
Victorious Titus, rue the tears I shed,
A mother's tears in passion for her son:
And if thy sons were ever dear to thee,
O, think my son to be as dear to me!
Sufficeth not that we are brought to Rome,
To beautify thy triumphs and return,
Captive to thee and to thy Roman yoke,
But must my sons be slaughter'd in the streets,
For valiant doings in their country's cause?
O, if to fight for king and commonweal
Were piety in thine, it is in these.
Andronicus, stain not thy tomb with blood:
Wilt thou draw near the nature of the gods?
Draw near them then in being merciful:
Sweet mercy is nobility's true badge:
Thrice noble Titus, spare my first-born son.

Titus Andronicus
William Shakespeare

Play
40+
Dramatic
Classical

Tamora, in her attempt to drive Titus mad, disguises herself as Revenge.

Know, thou sad man, I am not Tamora;
She is thy enemy, and I thy friend:
I am Revenge: sent from the infernal kingdom,
To ease the gnawing vulture of thy mind,
By working wreakful vengeance on thy foes.
Come down, and welcome me to this world's light;
Confer with me of murder and of death:
There's not a hollow cave or lurking-place,
No vast obscurity or misty vale,
Where bloody murder or detested rape
Can couch for fear, but I will find them out;
And in their ears tell them my dreadful name,
Revenge, which makes the foul offender quake.

The Tragedy of Jane Shore

Nicholas Rowe

Play
30s
Dramatic
Classical

Jane Shore, once the favorite mistress of Edward IV, has now fallen on hard times. When her friend suggests she seek pity from the Duke of Gloucester and others who forced her into poverty, Jane replies.

Why should I think that man will do for me
What yet he never did for wretches like me?
Mark by what partial justice we are judged;
Such is the fate unhappy women find,
And such the curse entailed upon our kind,
That man, the lawless libertine, may rove
Free and unquestioned through the wilds of love
While woman, sense and nature's easy fool,
If poor, weak woman swerve from virtue's rule,
If, strongly charmed, she leaves the thorny way,
And in the softer paths of pleasure stray;
Ruin ensues, reproach and endless shame,
And one false step entirely damns her fame,
In vain with tears the loss she may deplore,
In vain look back to what she was before;
She sets, like stars that fall, to rise no more.

Twelfth Night
William Shakespeare

Play
20s
Comic
Classical

Because she dressed as a man to survive, Viola has a female suitor who has professed her love. Viola takes a moment to appreciate the absurdity of her situation.

Disguise, I see, thou are a wickedness,
Wherein the pregnant enemy does much.
How easy it is for the proper-false
In women's waxen hearts to set their forms!
Alas, our frailty is the cause, not we!
For such as we are made of, such we be.
How will this fadge? my master loves her dearly;
And I, poor monster, fond as much on him;
And she, mistaken, seems to dote on me.
What will become of this? As I am man,
My state is desperate for my master's love;
As I am woman,—now alas the day—
What thriftless signs shall poor Olivia breathe!
O time! thou must untangle this, not I;
It is too hard a knot for me to untie!

The Two Noble Kinsmen

William Shakespeare and John Fletcher

Play
20s
Dramatic
Classical

A prince has proposed to the jailer's daughter, but she has fallen in love with a prisoner and vows to arrange his escape.

But in my heart was Palamon, and there,
Lord, what a coil he keeps! To hear him
Sing in an evening, what a heaven it is!
And yet his songs are sad ones. Fairer spoken
Was never gentleman; when I come in
To bring him water in a morning, first
He bows his noble body, then salutes me, thus:
"Fair, gentle maid, good morrow; may thy goodness
Get thee a happy husband." Once he kissed me;
I loved my lips the better ten days after—
Would he would do so every day! He grieves much,
And me as much to see his misery.
What should I do to make him know I love him?
For I would fain enjoy him. Say I ventured
To set him free? What says the law then? Thus much
For the law, or kindred! I will do it?
And this night, or tomorrow, he shall love me.

The Two Noble Kinsmen

William Shakespeare and John Fletcher

Play
20s
Dramatic
Classical

*The jailer's daughter, a fugitive for helping her lover escape
from jail, watches helplessly from shore as a ship sinks.*

I am very cold, and all the stars are out, too,
The little stars and all, that look like aglets.
The sun has seen my folly. Palamon!
Alas, no; he's in heaven. Where am I now?
Yonder's the sea, and there's a ship; how't tumbles!
And there's a rock lies watching under water;
Now, now, it beats upon it; now, now, now,
There's a leak spring, a sound one; how they cry!
Spoon her before the wind, you'll lose all else;
Up with a course or two, and tack about, boys.
Good night, good night, you're gone. I am very hungry.
Would I could find a fine frog; he would tell me
News from all parts o'th' world; then would I make
A carrack of a cockleshell, and sail
By east and north-east to the King of the Pygmies,
For he tells fortunes rarely. Now my father,
Twenty to one, is trussed up in a trice
Tomorrow morning; I'll never say a word.

Uncle Vanya

Anton Chekhov
Translated by Marian Fell

Play
27
Seriocomic
Classical

Considering her friend's unrequited love for Dr. Astroff, Helena confronts her own feelings.

I can understand how the poor child feels. She lives here in this desperate loneliness with no one around her except these color-less shadows that go mooning about talking nonsense and knowing nothing except that they eat, drink and sleep. Among them appears from time to time this Dr. Astroff, so different, so handsome, so interesting, so charming. It is like seeing the moon rise on a dark night. Oh, to surrender oneself to his embrace! To lose oneself in his arms! I am a little in love with him myself!

Yes . . . I am lonely without him, and when I think of him I smile. That Uncle Vanya says I have the blood of a nixie in my veins: "Give rein to your nature for once in your life!"

Perhaps it is right that I should. Oh, to be free as a bird, to fly away from all your sleepy faces and your talk and forget that you have existed at all!

But I am a coward. I am afraid; my conscience torments me. He comes here every day now. I can guess why, and feel guilty already; I should like to fall on my knees at Sonia's feet and beg her forgiveness, and weep.

Uncle Vanya

Anton Chekhov
Translated by Marian Fell

Play
20s-30s
Dramatic
Classical

Sonia works herself to a desperate pitch as she tells of being in love with a man who doesn't know she's alive.

(Looking in a mirror.) I'm homely, no getting around it. What? I have pretty hair? That's what they always tell a homely woman. "You have pretty hair, nice eyes." You know, I've been in love with Dr. Michail Lvovitch for six years. I love him more than my own mother. Every waking moment I hear the sound of his voice, feel the touch of his hand. I keep watching the door, hoping he'll come in. Here, for instance, I come to you just so I can talk about him. He's out here every day now, but he doesn't give me a tumble. It's killing me! Tearing me up inside! I don't have any hope anymore, none! God, give me strength! I was awake all night—praying. I approach him repeatedly, talk to him, looking into his eyes . . . I've no pride, I can't control myself. Yesterday I lost control completely and Uncle Vanya, I love him. All the servants know it. Everybody knows! But he doesn't know I'm alive.

The Wild Duck

Henrik Ibsen

Play
Teen
Dramatic
Classical

Her father has just discovered that Hedwig is not, in fact, his daughter. His love for her—and the wild duck that they nurture— immediately turns to hate.

Daddy! Daddy! Don't go away from me. He'll never come back to us again. I think I'm going to die of all this. What have I done to him? Mother, why doesn't Daddy want to see me any more? I think I know what it is. Perhaps I'm not Daddy's real child. And now perhaps he has found it out. I've read about that sort of thing. But I think he might be just as fond of me for all that. Almost more. The wild duck was sent us as a present too, and I'm tremendously fond of that, just the same. The poor wild duck! He can't bear to look at that any more, either. Just think he wanted to wring its neck. I say a prayer for the wild duck every night and ask that it shall be protected from death and everything bad. I taught myself to say my prayers because there was a time when Daddy was ill and had leeches on his neck and said he was lying at death's door. So I said a prayer for him when I'd gone to bed. And I've gone on with it ever since. I thought I'd better put in the wild duck too, because she was so delicate at first. And now you say I should sacrifice the wild duck to prove my love for Daddy. I will try it. I will ask Grandfather to shoot the wild duck for me.

CONTEMPORARY
MONOLOGUES

2.5 Minute Ride

Lisa Kron

Play
30s+
Seriocomic
Contemporary

Lisa's father, an infirm Holocaust survivor, insists on riding the big roller coaster at Cedar Point amusement park—an event that Lisa and her friend Mary must document.

At the entrance to the Magnum there are signs all over which say under no circumstances is this ride suitable for people who are elderly, diabetic or have heart conditions. I look at my father. He can't read the sign because, in addition to having all the conditions listed, he is also legally blind. (. . .)

Under no circumstances would they let us take a video camera on a roller coaster, but one of the girls told us that Mary could go up the exit stairs and shoot from the platform on the other side. When she got there, though, they gave her a hard time and she was really pissed off because these little high school amusement park girls were getting all snippy with her and making her stand in the sun, and she already had that kind of aggravated look that lesbians get in amusement parks in Ohio. So, she told me that I would have to go first and convince the girls to let her onto the exit platform. I found a method that worked pretty well, actually. I'd say, "Can my friend shoot here?" And the girls would say, "Well . . ." And I'd say, "We're doing a documentary video about my father. He's a seventy-four-year-old, blind, diabetic, Holocaust survivor with a heart condition." And they'd say, "Oooh. OK." It's painfully easy to place the weight of the world right on a teenage girl's shoulders.

After Math

Jonathan Dorf

Play
Teen
Dramatic
Contemporary

Emmet has disappeared, and every student has a different idea about what happened to him, including this "artsy looking" student.

(Standing in front of a wall mural at school.) Check out this mural. Yeah—take a second.

(Beat.) It's called the Unity Mural. You know, like peace and love, flowers in your hair, lighters in the air—you know. (. . .)

Emmett did this part. It looks all shiny, happy people like the rest of the mural. The student polishing the apple for the teacher, a study group in the library that's one of those Disney movies: white kid, black—African-American—kid, Latino kid, Asian kid—two boys, two girls. It's trippy how he does it, 'cause he's got four different study groups—there's hardly any books in the library there's so many study groups—it's like what's the point of it being in the library? And each study group is a different combination. Black guy, white guy, Asian girl, Latin girl. Black girl, white girl, Asian guy, Latin guy. You get the idea. Disney.

(Beat.)

But if you look really close—

(SHE points at something very small in the mural.) —and it's not just way small, it's upside down—if you know what you're looking for, it's there. The principal going through a student's locker. A cloud of smoke in the bathroom filled with

unflushed toilets. Books covered in cobwebs 'cause they're older than the teachers. A kid being shoved into a garbage can for being . . . maybe just for being.

(Beat.)

It's like those animators who slip that one frame into the G-rated movie, or "I Am the Walrus" played backward. Emmett was the Walrus. I don't think the school liked that.

The Air That I Breathe

Theresa Carilli

Original Monologue
Early 20s
Seriocomic
Contemporary

Sonnie is a sweet, butch lesbian with few aspirations.

Mindy seems a bit angry at me today. We've been arguing a lot lately but I think its because we spend way too much time together. Not only do we live together, but we work together at the High Faludin' Café over on Wilbur Street. Sometimes, we even have the same shifts. Like tonight for example, she's been here since three this afternoon and I got here around five. I always kiss her when I arrive and I know it makes her sort of mad because even though everyone knows we're lovers, she likes to pretend it's a secret. We work with this other dyke who calls herself Lassie, something which I think is really embarrassing but she thinks it rocks. I'm not sure how she got this nickname but she has it tattooed all over her body. She says it has something to do with being Scottish and I have to be honest, that reference is lost on me. I can understand being proud of your ethnicity and all but I just cannot understand taking on the name of a doggie heroine. She's short and stocky, large breasted, bluish green eyes and actually if it weren't for her nickname, I'd think she was sexy.

Alchemy of Desire/ Dead Man's Blues

Caridad Svich

Play
Late teens
Seriocomic
Contemporary

Miranda, a spirited young woman, speaks to Simone who fishes off a riverbank.

My grammy'd take me. When I was little
She's the one did the actual fishin.
I'd just watch her. *(Pulls out a cigarette.)* Smoke? (. . .)
She'd just smile . . . sit there . . . fish.
She'd smoke, too.
Not cigarettes, but a big ol' cigar bout this thick.
You should've seen the smoke she'd blow out of that thing.
Swirls and swirls of it, like chimney smoke.
And it smelled, too. (. . .)
I hated it. All of it. The cigars. Everythin.
Felt like it was a punishment every time I had to go out
With her. Grammy and her goddam tobacco.
But after awhile, I don't know how it occurred,
the smell of that tobacco became like heaven itself. (. . .)
Rollin' and lightin' up. Smokin' and castin' a line.
It was all of a piece with Grammy.
I'd sit there, wallowin' in the smell,
swear all angels had come down to pay us a visit.
Used to try to catch the rings of smoke with my mouth,
Like some sort of weird human kind of fish.

I must've caught a hundred rings one time. One hundred.
I swear, it was the best part of goin' fishin'.
'N fact, for the longest time,
that's what I thought fishin' was:
just something you did to go smoking.

Alchemy of Desire/
Dead Man's Blues

Caridad Svich

Play
Late 20s-early 30s
Dramatic
Contemporary

Simone has just lost her husband, Jamie.

Truth is, I married him.
When you come right down to it,
I'm the one who did the marryin.
Jamie just fell into it.
'n fact, I'd say we sort of fell into each other:
He didn't know what he was doin,
and I was still burnin with the memory
of havin made love in his car.

It's a strange thing: desire.
It makes you do things for no other reason
than a mighty feelin you can't even put your finger on
says you *got* to do it.
  . . . Strange.

Haven't cleaned up the house yet.
Haven't even been in the house,
not for more than an hour or two at a time, not since the wake.
I don't wanna go in there.
It still smells like fried chicken.
'n what stuff he had is in there, too.
It's too pitiful to sit around, touch it. . . wouldn't know what to do.

I sleep in the yard.

All Stories Are True

John Edgar Wideman

Short Story
60+
Dramatic
Contemporary

A mother laments the changes in the neighborhood's young people, and in her son.

That's how they do us. Steal anything and everything. Stained-glass windows out the church. I worry about one of them getting into the house.

Sorry-assed junkies.

Dope turns them crazy. Knock you down as soon as look at you. Kids you've watched grow up around here. I don't believe they intend to hurt anybody, but when that sickness is down on them, my, my, my, they'll do anything. I shudder when I think of your brother crazy that way. Him hurting someone or someone hurting him. Those so-called friends of his he'd bring home. Yes ma'am and no ma'am me and all the time I know their dope eyes counting up what they could come back and steal. Tommy knew it, too. God have mercy on me for saying this about my own son, but I believe now that's why he brought some of them around. To steal from me.

American Standard

Jonathan Joy

Play
20s-30s
Seriocomic
Contemporary

*Faith, a small-town, country girl with big city flair, lectures
two lecherous senatorial candidates about political and personal priorities.*

Stop! Neither one of you is really interested in what I have to
say. It's just your pathetic attempt to engage someone else in a
conversation on your favorite topic—yourselves. Don't you
ever talk about anything else? When was the last time either of
you were doing anything other than promoting yourselves and
your agenda? You spend your entire lives crammed into little
offices, pouring through documents, or better yet, having someone do it for you, making decisions that affect the people that
you supposedly represent. And at the end of the day what
really matters is to try to get it all done by five o'clock so you
can hit the bar in time for happy hour and flirt with the cute
young interns. And why do you do it? Because you love the
power. You live off the excitement of beating the other political
party like you were playing a god damned football game or
something. Then, every couple of years you come back out here
and try to convince all of us dumb country bumpkins that
you've done great things for the state but you can do so much
more if we just give you two more years. And after you win
we never see you again. And you wonder why people hate

politicians? Well, there you go. I hope that answers any subsequent questions you may have had. (*Silence.*) And stop sending me gifts, both of you. You don't know anything about women either.

And by His Hand, Lightning

Amy Unsworth

Play
Late teens
Dramatic
Contemporary

*Vesta, daughter of Saturn and Rhea, levies a curse on her parents
after slipping the baby, Zeus, to safety.*

Father, I live yet, a handmaiden to my mother
at her birthing bed. When my brothers slip
scarlet from her womb you catch them
a starving man devouring fish—
flesh raw, still wet with sea and salt.

Their heads are pomegranates in your great palms.
You plunge your fingers through their soft crowns,
greedy for a delicacy the gods will not even allow a king.
Even when you have pressed the wine sop of muscle
to your lips, you hunger yet.

And with her fruitless fecund womb still distended,
you fall to my mother's robed body, mad
to her seeping breasts. And she nurses you,
with the milk meant for my infant brother,
nourishes you while I gather his bones. Murderer,

tonight while you gorged, from my mother's guttered
womb, I stole a second son, unseen. Wrapped
with the ruin of our brothers, in the rags and refuse,

this son will consume you. He will bring forth
an awesome birthing, son after son, sprung

full grown from the belly of your gluttony
from the wracked womb of jealously and fear.
And by his hand, lightning, and the thunder
of your wrong will roar through all generations.

And Now a Word from Our Sponsor

Clinton A. Johnston

Original Monologue
20+
Comic
Contemporary

The announcement you don't want to hear in the store you already hate.

Attention shoppers. This is your Super-Mart radio network reminding you that "We've got a lotta' great things in store." (*Drastic change in tone.*) So, buy stuff!

That's right, you heard me! Buy stuff! Move your flabby, fat asses and buy stuff! We got stuff to buy, so buy stuff! I'm not here for my health and neither are you. You're here to buy stuff! So stop dicking around and buy stuff! Hello! I don't see you buying enough stuff! We got lots of stuff here people! We got a whole store of stuff that you could be buying right now! We got items on sale. We got items at reduced prices. We got fresh, hoity-toity foods made at the deli. We've got bread baked fresh this morning. Our meat department has real meat! We've got cute little plastic crap for your kids. We've got cute, little, crappy, plastic containers for you! Get it? We've got stuff you can put stuff in! We've got seasonal stuff! We've got magazines and books. We've got stuff in the aisles, stuff on top of the aisles, stuff at the checkout stand! Hey! Things are stuff all over! Buy more stuff! Buy stuff! Buy stuff! Buy stuff!

And the Winner Is
David-Matthew Barnes

Play
20s
Seriocomic
Contemporary

Tracy disses her fellow nominees in a made-for-TV moment.

Listen up, you little star*fuckers!* My name is Tracy Morrison
and I'm here because I was nominated for my performance in
Sorrow Is My Sister. Now, if y'all wanna be *nasty* about this,
then I can be nasty. First of all, April Newton—everyone that I
know has slept with your husband at least a dozen times—(. . .)
And Pauline Emerson (. . .) Your movies are almost as bad as
your nose job—(. . .) you triflin' ho! You lay on a doorstep
faster than the mornin' newspaper. And Rachel Riley—for some
God-awful reason, some dumb ass put you in a movie and told
you that you can act. *Shhheeeit.* (. . .) I could make one of
your movies with ten dollars and a hooker from Harlem. And
Danielle Taylor—you little drunk bitch—(. . .) In a year, you'll
be burned out, used up, and doing infomercials. I, myself,
worked three jobs to put myself through college. I've studied
every aspect of actin' you can possibly imagine. (. . .) It took
me eleven years to get a part in a film—and now that I'm
here—I'm not going anywhere! I got an agent. I got a manager.
I got a lawyer. I got a publicist. I've got a personal *mothah
fuckin'* assistant. And it's about time. I deserve all of this—
because unlike the four of you *dirty tramps*—(. . .) I *care*
about the movies I make and not the size of my bank account.
So if the four of you cannot maintain yourselves like the decent

young women that God intended y'all to be, then step aside, because I *can* and I *will*. It's not about box office. It's not about power. It's not about having your face on every trashy magazine in America. It's about givin' somethin' to the world—and believe you me, I've got plenty to give. Now, get that camera rollin', because I am ready for my interview.

Angry Young Man
Daniel Trujillo

Play
20s
Seriocomic
Contemporary

Cecilia, a New York actress, disappeared from a party after learning her big break into movies fell through. She's returned this morning to her hyper-principled boyfriend, Frank, ready to join him in artistic exile with a Nebraskan political theater company. Frank doubts the sincerity of her new commitment.

I lost the part, lost patience for the losses,
Lost all desire to please the Hollywood bosses,
But how to lose your doubt that I'm sincere?
I got no clue. Frank, I didn't come here
To prove myself. I'm here because we could
Still salvage some small scrap of common good.
Yes, I was down with that commercial coven.
I don't hate heat. I jumped into the oven.
I didn't move to N-Y-C to jerk
A tap, to temp, to wait, I came to work.
Not like those ingénues who go entomb
Themselves in someone's sixth-floor showcase room.
I'm losing count of my associates
Who've burnt their youth like so many cigarettes;
And wasted talents, drunks, how many eaten
Inside because they let themselves get beaten?
The terrible truth is that it's still a colder
Climate out there when girls start getting older.
I'm running out of time, and when it's done

I need one memory underneath the sun.
Perhaps I'm weak or ignorant. I guess
My passion's nothing more and nothing less;
But pity, praise, ignore, despise or taunt
My craving, I will get the life I want.
And that, I think, is what you want from me:
The nerve to grab for opportunity.

Animal Husbandry

Laura Zigman

Novel
30s-40s
Seriocomic
Contemporary

*An animal behaviorist finds something in her research to
explain her failed relationship.*

[I]t was just like every other morning I'd had since being
dumped.

I woke up before the alarm. I remembered a dream I'd had
about Ray. (A wild boar was chasing him around the green-
room. Was I the wild boar?) I recalled a few choice aspects of
our relationship (his washboard stomach, his bad-love-poetry
E-mails, his impeccable taste in cheesy vacation souvenirs).
Which made me cry. Which made me mad.

Which propelled me into the shower, and then to make coffee,
and then to sit at the kitchen table smoking cigarettes until I
realized that nothing would become of me unless I got dressed
and dragged my ass to work.

Little did I know that when I opened the science section of the
newspaper at my desk an hour later, I would find the nugget,
the germ, the essence of what would become my obsession over
the next year: a reference to the mating preferences of bulls
buried in an article on human male behavior. (. . .)

The Coolidge Effect was the technical name for it—it—the need
to provide bulls with multiple cows for mating. Multiple cows
for mating.

Anne
Adam Szymkowicz

Play
20s
Dramatic
Contemporary

Cassandra, one of Anne's multiple personalities, describes the day she was created due to her father's sexual abuse.

On the day I was born it was snowy it was cloudy it was rainy it was hailing it was a 30 percent chance of flowers it was coming down going up not a cloud in the sky it was seventy mostly cloudy it was tossing and turning on the sea it was running up and down the stairs cause I remember cause I was there on the day I was born.

On the day I was born we all had ice cream because your tummy hurt. Hank had mint chocolate chip. Maxine had rum punch. We had vanilla in a big sugar cone.

On the day I was born I came out head first from between your child legs. The human body, the human brain, the human faculties adapt. I am opposable thumbs. I am camouflage, extra eyelids, extra teeth.

I will be you when you can't. I will be your voice, your body. I will take the knife for you. I will take it and take it and take it. And I will like it, because you won't.

Or when you are hugging the wall, in the punch bowl watching the other kids dancing close, I will go up to the scariest boy. I will tell him to dance with me and if he says no, I will kick him hard.

Approximating Mother

Kathleen Tolan

Play
Teens
Seriocomic
Contemporary

Jen's story of her visit to a social worker gushes forth.

[S]he told me I would regret it if I had an abortion and I said I
regretted this whole thing but that's what I wanted to do and I
didn't want to have a baby, I wanted to finish high school and
stuff and she said if I wasn't ready to be a mother there were
many wonderful couples who would love a baby and I said,
well that's fine but I don't want to do that so she said (. . .) I
should think about how I'd feel if my parents had decided not
to have me and I said, "Huh?" And she said she knew this
must be a very scary and confusing time for me and I should
know she was my friend and I said I didn't think so and then
she got really nasty because she knew I could see right through
her and she started screeching, "Go ahead, kill the baby. Kill
the baby. See how it makes you feel." And some day I'd wish I
had a baby, wouldn't I and I said I don't know what you're
talking about, let me out of here and went home and went up
to my room and was just shaking and crying and I told my
mom I had the flu and just stayed up there for a couple of days
and finally I told my mom I was pregnant. And then everybody
completely freaked out and here I am.

At Swim, Two Boys
Jamie O'Neill

Novel
60+
Dramatic
Contemporary

1916, Ireland. The formidable Aunt Eva, matriarch of the MacMurrough family, makes plans to reintroduce her young nephew into society. He has recently served jail time in England for "gross indecency" and is now staying with her in Dublin.

Let us dismiss your embarrass with the English. A small clarification is all that is required. How the English (. . .) concocted the charges against you. You will find society only too willing for so happy an éclaircissement. The world of affairs awaits you, my boy. I intend you shall enter it and prosper. (. . .)

We shall begin with the garden fete. Don't glower so, Anthony. You know perfectly well one cannot have one's nephew staying without an announcement. It would not do. (. . .)

Whatever has happened, we are still MacMurroughs, and I will not have you shut in your room the day (. . .). The garden fete will mark your return. I shall invite all the leading families. The nationalist ones, naturally. They will see a bright likely young man leading local youth in patriotic song and everyone shall be charmed. For you are a charming boy when you wish to be. You have élan, you have éclat, you have breeding. And you shall marry. (. . .) Of course you shall marry. Did you think I would allow our name to die on account of some foolishness in London? I have never heard such a thing.

At the Salon
Maureen A. Connolly

Original Monologue
40-50s
Comic
Contemporary

Bernice looks at herself in the beauty salon mirror. As she talks to the hairdresser, also visible in the mirror, she fusses.

(Holding up hair on one side of her head.) I don't like this. *(Holding up hair on the other side.)* And I don't like this.

Fix it.

Please.

(Points to the back of her head.) This is OK, though. Isn't it? I like the length and the line.

More color. I need more color. Nothing drastic, though.

I've had bad, bad experiences with color. Wrong color and you'd think I have jaundice. Like a preemie that has to sleep under fluorescent lights.

Right color—my eyes stand out. Can't explain that one. But I know when it's right.

(More fussing with hair.) I used to go to Angelina. At Shear Madness. Somebody saw the future when they named that place.

It's my own fault. I suppose for staying with Angelina too long.

I tried Salon *Uno*. Ha! Doesn't take long before *U-Know* better than to go back there.

I heard you're great. A miracle worker, they say. So, I danced on in here.

What do you think?

What do you want to do with me?

Autumn Come Early

William J. Burns

Play
30s
Dramatic
Contemporary

In repetitious, lyrical patois, Monica tosses out her drunk husband.

Jimmy, I warned you! I told you! Don't never come home! How many times I gotta say, Jimmy? Don't never come home! Not never again! Not past midnight! Smellin' like a brewery! (. . .)

Stinkin' like fish an' seaweed an' stale beer! Sweet Jesus. Stinkin' of all o' them cheap cigars! Stinkin' like somethin' that even the river don't want! (. . .)

An' then you come stumblin' around in the dark. Stumblin'! Knockin' stuff over. Scarin' the girls half to death! (. . .)

An' then you come crawlin' in bed like a snake! Like a snake, Jimmy! Like somethin' that's cold. Like somethin' that give up its soul. Like somethin' with scales instead o' skin. (. . .)

It's like sleepin' with somethin' that's dead, Jimmy. Like sleepin' with somethin' decayin'. Like sleepin' with somethin' that ought'a be buried! You hear me, Jimmy? (. . .)

Jimmy! I did! I put up with it long enough. Now get outta here. Get outta here right now! Or I'm callin' the cops. I swear to God I'm callin' the cops! An' I mean it, Jimmy! You hear me? Now get outta here!

Baby in the Basement

David-Matthew Barnes

Play
Teen
Dramatic
Contemporary

A runaway has inadvertently interrupted the suicide of a young man hiding in an abandoned warehouse. As she describes to the dying young man what their dream home will look like, she begins to take the remaining pills herself.

It's yellow, with shutters and trim around the windows. And there's flowers. Yellow roses and white carnations and even some daffodils. It's a beautiful house. It's not too fancy. It's simple. Like us. Our friends will come over and we'll feed them a ton of food and we'll play some cool music and we can dance. And in the summer, we'll save up our money and we'll go to Paris. We'll take pictures and we will send postcards. Postcards to our families. Maybe they will miss us while we're away on our vacation. *(Pauses, a realization.)* They won't miss me. They won't even realize I'm gone. My father will give his sermon. My mother will ignore me. My sister will damage her baby. Leave her in a basement. Just like this one. I would never do that to my baby. I would keep her warm and safe. I haven't even picked out a name for her yet. What do you think I should name my baby? What do you think of Melissa? Do you like that name? I always liked the name Rachel. It's a pretty name. No. I will definitely name my baby Shelley. She was a good friend to me. I guess we got a plan, after all. *(Pauses.)* You're a sweet guy. You've got a cute smile. *(Pauses.)* I can't wait to see Paris with you.

The Beard of Avon
Amy Freed

Play
20s
Comic
Contemporary

Spoken by Anne Hathaway, wife of William Shakespeare.

Ooooh, LONDON! Well, life is certainly strange. 'Twould never be believed in a FICTION that my own husband might not penetrate my disguise. Oooh, what adventures have I had! Once arrived in Colin's rags, I went to see my cousin Lucy, a bawd about town. (*A MAN dressed as LUCY enters with an assistant and an armful of clothes and a hairpiece.*) She took me in and thrilling to my device, outfitted me in her own sluttish fashion. (*Fast, festive music. Through the following, LUCY disrobes ANNE of Colin's rags, snaps her into pieces of costume appropriate for a woman of lively morals, including a corset, a hairpiece, choker, and gloves.*) Such THINGS she has! That push you IN where you go OUT, and puff you OUT where you don't, actually. Paints as white as poison and rouge as red as roses! Cheek patches, corsets, chokers, and gloves . . . shoes that make you taller than your own dumpy self—for once in my life I'm slender! (*Transformation is now completed.*) No wonder why my husband loves the theater! I never want to go home again—and just look at this hair! (*LUCY and ASSISTANT exit with rags. ANNE looks at herself enthralled She's gorgeous, comic and dangerous, in a kind of "Carmen" way. She tears up.*) Had I only been a man, I might have been . . . an actress.

Bee-luther-hatchee

Thomas Gibbons

Play
30+
Dramatic
Contemporary

Libby luxuriates in a word that puts her in touch with a salient childhood memory.

My mama used to use that word when I was a little girl. Lord knows where she picked it up—I never heard it from anyone else. I loved the sound of it, the feelin' it made inside me. And I'd misbehave just to get her to say it. She knew what I was up to—it was a game we played. She'd look at me with big, wide eyes. If you ain't careful, she'd say, you gone end up in Bee-luther-hatchee.

Where's that, Mama, I'd ask. Is that someplace like hell? Never you mind, she'd say, and give me a kiss.

But once, I remember, she told me somethin' different. Her face got sad, and her voice was quiet and far off.

Hell ain't the last stop on the track, she said. Most folks think so, but they're wrong. After the passengers get off, after the conductor turns the lights out and leaves . . . you just stay on the train, gal. Bee-luther-hatchee is the next stop after hell.

Bee-luther-hatchee

Thomas Gibbons

Play
30+
Dramatic
Contemporary

Libby's mother has told her that Bee-luther-hatchee is "the next stop after hell." Libby relives a moment that takes her to that place.

I heard the door of the car open and the conductor come in to collect the tickets. I sat real still and tried to be invisible. Usually that ain't too hard with white folks. Except when it comes to money—then you shine like the sun.

He stopped next to me and said, Can I see your ticket? I don't have one, I said. Not lookin' at him. You can buy one from me, he said. He had a nice voice. I said, I don't have the money.

Come with me, he said. Come on. His voice still sounded nice, but there was somethin' different in it.

All the people in the car were starin' at me, I could tell. No one was talkin'. I stood up and followed him all the way up the aisle into the next car . . . the kind that had private compartments.

Please, mister, I said. I know I done wrong. Just let me get off at the next stop. He grabbed my wrist and started lookin' through the windows of the compartments.

You're hurtin' me, I told him. He opened a door and pushed me into an empty compartment. He pulled the shade down on the window. Then he turned around and hit me. Not real hard . . . just enough to *let me know.*

And he said, Since you can't buy a ticket, you'll have to earn your ride.

Big Boy
Theresa M. Carilli

Original Monologue
30+
Dramatic
Contemporary

A prizefighter's daughter recalls the family's home life.

See this crack on the wall? This was one of the Christmas cracks. This one here was an Easter crack. When I was a kid, Mom used to hang my artwork over the cracks that Dad used to make—either with his fist or head. After awhile there were so many cracks, Mom stopped putting up my artwork. It looked more natural that way. He'd get mad and he'd ram his head into the wall. Sometimes, but seldom, his fist. And if he was really mad, he'd get down on his hands and knees and smash his head into the metal radiators until it would bleed. (. . .)

I remember the day Dad came home after gambling the house away. It was some business deal he said. But we all knew. He turned white, broke all the windows in the house, took some downers that the doctor prescribed for his nerves and then he split to "jump off a bridge." It was Christmas Eve. The police found him on the bridge and brought him home. Mom would have left him if he didn't have a nervous breakdown. Mom would have left him if she weren't afraid he would kill her.

Big-Butt Girls, Hard-Headed Women

Rhodessa Jones

Play
30
Dramatic
Contemporary

Regina Brown, incarcerated, holds forth.

Everybody and anybody will use you so you best get to using first. I learned early, a man or a woman ain't nothin' but a plaything. I tell them all, "It's like the lotto, Baby. You got to be in it to win it." Later for all that "Ooh, Baby" this and "Ooh, Baby" that. I believe in action, so you best got on with the A team. Like Tyrone, he's in love with me, always has been, and I can understand that. But I told him, "I was born a full-grown woman, and it ain't about 'my woman this' and 'my woman that.' I'm my own woman." But, like a lot of men, he don't want to listen. Wanted to control me . . . thought he was my daddy. My daddy's dead, Baby. And my mama raised me to be strong and on my own. He got all mad, 'cause he wasn't ready for the real deal. Brought some other girl, some Lily-Lunchmeat-lookin' bitch I don't know, home! I told him, "Hey, if sister girl can hang, it's all in the family." Thought he was gonna work my nerves with that shit. And now who's crying? Tyrone. Because I'm carrying another man's baby. And that man ain't even important. (. . .) I am a prostitute, straight up. I decided a long time ago, wasn't no man gonna tell me what to do. I'm a full-grown woman, straight up and down. Or my name ain't Regina Brown.

Bird Germs

Eric R. Pfeffinger

Play
30
Seriocomic
Contemporary

Ellen Birnbaum talks to her therapist.

We were watching TV! OK? Dad was gone, I was in charge, we
were watching TV. Dolores won the rock-paper-scissors, so
instead of *Mork and Mindy* we were watching, I don't even
remember, *Stowaway*. Or *The Littlest Rebel*, who knows. Dad
was at one of his, you know, things . . . a socialist rally. I
remembered that we'd let Eugene out before dinner, so I went
to the door and let him in, and he runs in and he's got this
thing in his mouth. Probably just a stick, but I also remembered
the time he was eating his own poop, so I was like "Hmmm."
We're trying to get the thing, and he thinks this is a great game,
chase-the-dog-with-the-thing-in-his-mouth. Then Dolores goes,
"It's a bird!" And it was a bird, or most of a bird. And we're
both like "Ewwwwww!" and then Eugene's chasing us, which
he thinks is even a better game, and I'm thinking "What if he
swallows it?" which, at least then it's gone. But it's pretty big
and there's a beak involved and at least one leg and it's not
food, it's a toy to him, it's a new hobby as far as Eugene is concerned. And Dolores is running around the living room shriek-
ing "Bird germs! Bird germs!" Dad's not home, of course, why
would Dad be home to deal with the bird when there's injustice
in the world. So we called the long-distance number Dad left
us, the number we're absolutely positively not supposed to call

except in an emergency . . . (*Dials phone, squeals excitedly into the receiver.*) Bird germs bird germs Eugene's got a dead bird and it's in the house and we're pretty sure it has germs . . . ! Ohmygod ohmygod it's coming over here! Don't let it touch the Fritos!

The Blacks, A Clown Show

Jean Genet

Translated by Bernard Frechtman

Play
20+
Dramatic
Contemporary

1960. Before a jury of white-masked blacks, black players enact the ritualistic murder of a white woman, then condemn the court itself. Shocking for its time, the play still holds up for its violent attack on the privileges of white society. Here, a player named Felicity calls for ceremonial rescue.

To my rescue, Negroes, all of you! Gentlemen of Timbuctoo, come in, under your white parasols! Stand over there. Tribes covered with gold and mud, rise up from my body, emerge! Tribes of the Rain and Wind, forward! Princes of the Upper Empires Princes of the bare feet and wooden stirrups, on your caparisoned horses, enter! Enter on horseback. Gallop in! Gallop in! Hop it! Hop it! Hop along! Negroes of the ponds, you who fish with your pointed beaks, enter! Negroes of the docks, of the factories, of the dives. Negroes of the Ford plant, Negroes of General Motors, and you, too, Negroes who braid rushes to encage crickets and roses, enter and remain standing! Conquered soldiers, enter. Conquering soldiers, enter. Crowd in. More. Lay your shields against the walls. You, too, who dig up corpses to suck the brains from skulls, enter unashamedly. You, tangled brother-sister, walking melancholy incest, come in. Barbarians, barbarians, barbarians, come along. I can't describe you all, nor even name you all, nor name your dead, your arms, your ploughs, but enter.

Blanca
Danny Hoch

Play
20s
Seriocomic
Contemporary

A young, pretty, twenty-something office worker stops by her friend's house to borrow shoes for a date with her boyfriend, Manny.

So he's Puerto Rican, right? And he's dark and his last name is Sorullo. So when people ask him, he always says Sorrulo. 'Cause he says he wants to work in business in Wall Street, and that nobody wants to hire a Sorullo. So I be telling him, "Manny, that's your last name, you can't do that." And he be getting angry at me like, "That's my last name, that's how it's pronounced!" And like, "You got it easier than me, Blanca, 'cause you're lighter than me, 'cause you're a woman." And I'm like, "Excuse me, I'm Puerto Rican too," right?

So it was the Puerto Rican Day Parade, and I had gotten us these T-shirts with the Puerto Rican flag in the front, and in the back there's a little coquí and it says, "Boricua and Proud." So you would think that he would be like, "Oh, thank you, Blanca, that's so sweet, I love you," right? Instead he starts screaming, "I'm not wearing this shit! I can't believe you got me this! It's ugly!" I was like, "Excuse me, it's not ugly." So he puts on a Ralph Lauren shirt. I was like, "Manny, you think somebody's hiring you for Wall Street at the Puerto Rican Day

Parade?" So he goes to me, "Look Blanca, I might be Puerto Rican, but I don't have to walk around looking like one." . . . I was like, "Excuse me. You think that people think that you Swedish? You Puerto Rican."

Bookends
Jonathan Dorf

Play
30s
Dramatic
Contemporary

Susan is an English professor.

Good morning. I am Professor Susan Harris, and the name
of this course *(Eric, looking like he's overslept, enters. Susan
pauses to watch him.)* is Shakespeare. It should be called
Shakespeare's plays, because we don't study his poetry. I don't
like all that sissy sonnet crap. Shakespeare, ladies and gentlemen, is about winners and losers. And whatever happens is
always the loser's fault. Richard II, consummate loser. Loses his
kingdom because he's too slow and pathetic to do anything. It's
his fault. Think about it. Why do we care about Richard? It's
ludicrous. In fact, I would propose that Richard is actually the
usurper and that Henry Bullingbrook was king all along.
Richard is, therefore, filler, and since there are already two
plays named after Henry IV, Richard II should be eliminated
entirely. However, the department is strongly against eliminat-
ing Richard II from the syllabus, so as a compromise we will
be reading only Henry's lines. *(Beat.)*

Give me a loser, ladies and gentlemen, and I will give you a
place to lay the blame. Did Richard III cry? Of course not. But
all those cowardly dukes and princes who committed suicide
and tried to frame him did. Richard III met death the way he

met life. With confidence. He went out a winner. Study his speeches with care. Memorize them. You will be tested on them. You will not be asked to remember the losers. You may discard them in literature as you should in life.

Broken Eggs

Eduardo Machado

Play
40+
Dramatic
Contemporary

Sonia Marquez Hernandez, a Cuban woman, shares her "Coming to America" story with her daughter.

When I first got here . . . I got lost, I tried to ask an old man for directions. I could not find the right words to ask him the directions. He said to me, "What's wrong with you, lady, somebody give you a lobotomy?" I repeated that word over and over to myself, "lobotomy, lobotomy, lo-bo-to-meee!" I looked it up. It said an insertion into the brain, for relief, of tension. I remembered people who had been lobotomized, that their minds could not express anything, they could feel nothing. They looked numb, always resting, then I realized that the old man was right. (. . .) So I decided never to communicate or deal with this country again. Mimi, I don't know how to go back to my country. He made me realize that to him, I looked like a freak.

Caitlyn

Steve Mitchell

Original Monologue
12-15
Dramatic
Contemporary

Caitlyn recalls the moment when music entered her body and her life.

When I was a little kid, I mean like five or six,
my grandma would take me to plays and concerts.
Sometimes I liked it, sometimes I got bored.

One time we were at this concert, a man playing piano,
and we were sitting right on the front row.
I guess I was restless. And I guess he noticed.

So, after he finished the first piece,
he came over to the front of the stage, he looked down at me
—this is right in the middle of the concert now—
and asked me to come up on stage with him.
And I did.
He took my hand and led me over.
He had me sit right up under the piano, right between the legs.

At first I was nervous, with the audience and the lights
but once he started to play, I didn't notice the audience anymore.
It wasn't as loud as you'd think under there, but the floor trembled.
I didn't have to listen, I could feel the music on my skin.

Carrie

Steve Lyons

Original Monologue
20s
Comic
Contemporary

Carrie is pregnant and way hormonal. She speaks to her husband, Norman.

The spirit of the ages is welling up within me. (*Carrie looks off into the distance as she begins her vision.*)

I remember . . . I remember, when I was eight years old, Roxy—our beagle terrier mix gave birth to five puppies. We had made up a special box for her to have her puppies in. Put a blanket in it. Some water. She never went in that box . . . until that day. Roxy didn't take any classes or read any books. Roxy just knew what to do. It was as if all time had stopped and it was just Roxy and me and three deep breaths, then puuuush. I was doing it with her. The world's first eight-year-old birthing coach. (*Carrie imitates the three deep breaths and push.*) At that moment, I thought that Roxy was the most powerful being in the universe. And you know what? At that moment, she was. (*Louder.*) I learned it all from you Roxy. (*Eight months pregnant, CARRIE struggles to rise, louder.*) You held the torch high that I might follow. (*Louder.*) I won't let you down Roxy. (*Louder.*) HANDS ACROSS THE SPECIES! (*To her feet.*) ROXY! (*Throws her head back, arms held in a V above her head, fists clenched.*) SISTERHOOD IS POWERFUL! (*She holds this pose a moment, then lets her arms drop to her side. Looks at Norman, regular, matter-of-fact voice:*) OK, let's go.

Cat on a Hot Tin Roof

Tennessee Williams

Play
Mid 20s
Dramatic
Contemporary

Maggie longs for her husband, Brick, to want her the way other men do.

You know, our sex life didn't just peter out in the usual way, it was cut off short, long before the natural time for it to, and it's going to revive again, just as sudden as that. I'm confident of it. That's what I'm keeping myself attractive for. For the time when you'll see me again like other men see me. Yes, like other men see me. They still see me, Brick, and they like what they see. Uh-huh. Some of them would give their—Look Brick! *(She stands before the long oval mirror, touches her breast and then her hips with her two hands.)* How high my body stays on me!—Nothing has fallen on me—not a fraction!

(Her voice is soft and trembling: a pleading child's. At this moment as he turns to glance at her—a look which is like a player passing a ball to another player, third down and goal to go—she has to capture the audience in a grip so tight that she can hold it till the first intermission without any lapse of attention.)

Other men still want me. My face looks strained, sometimes, but I've kept my figure as well as you've kept yours, and men admire it. I still turn heads on the street. Why, last week in

Memphis everywhere that I went men's eye burned holes in my clothes, at the country club and in restaurants and department stores, there wasn't a man I met or walked by that didn't just eat me up with his eyes and turn around when I passed him and look back at me. Why, at Alice's party for her New York cousins, the best-lookin' man in the crowd—followed me upstairs and tried to force his way in the powder room with me, followed me to the door and tried to force his way in!

Cat on a Hot Tin Roof
Tennessee Williams

Play
30s
Seriocomic
Contemporary

Maggie talks to Brick about their nieces and nephews, all no-neck monsters.

Yes, it's too bad because you can't wring their necks if they've got no necks to wring! Isn't that right honey? Yep, they're no-neck monsters, all no-neck people are monsters. (*Children shriek downstairs.*) Hear them? Hear them screaming? I don't know where their voice boxes are located since they don't have necks. (. . .) Big Daddy hadn't been at the table two minutes with those five no-neck monsters slobbering and drooling over their food before he threw down his fork an' shouted, "Fo' God's sake, Gooper, why don't you put them pigs at a trough in th' kitchen?"—Well, I swear, I simply could have diieed! Think of it, Brick, they've got five of them and number six is coming. They've brought the whole bunch down here like animals to display at a county fair. Why, they have those children doin' tricks all the time! "Junior, show Big Daddy how you do this, show Big Daddy how you do that, say your little piece fo' Big Daddy, Sister. Show your dimples, Sugar. Brother, show Big Daddy how you stand on your head!"—it goes on all the time, along with constant little remarks and innuendoes about the fact that you and I have not produced any children, are totally childless and therefore totally useless!—Of course it's comical but its also disgusting since it so obvious what they're up to!

Charming Billy

Alice McDermott

Novel
45+
Dramatic
Contemporary

Billy Lynch's family and friends have gathered at a small Bronx bar to comfort his widow, Maeve, whose thoughts we hear in this monologue. Billy was an alcoholic.

"If you knew Billy at all," he said, "then you loved him. He was just that type of guy."

And if you loved him, we all knew, you pleaded with him at some point. Or you drove him to AA, waited outside the church till the meeting was over, and drove him home again. Or you advanced him whatever you could afford so he could travel to Ireland to take the pledge. If you loved him, you took his car keys away, took his incoherent phone calls after midnight. You banished him from your house until he could show up sober. You saw the bloodied scraps of flesh he coughed up into his drinks. If you loved him, then you told him at some point that he was killing himself and felt the way his indifference ripped through your affection. You left work early to identify his body at the VA, and instead of being grateful that the ordeal was at long last over, you felt a momentary surge of joy as you turned away . . .

Cheater Catchers
Elizabeth L. Farris

Original Monologue
30s
Comic
Contemporary

A Private Investigator has a moment of truth.

She found me in the yellow pages. I call myself Cheater-Catchers.

They'd been together six years. In this business, I find 'em cheatin' all the time, no matter how long it's been.

So I got the history, every detail of the suspicious behavior. You know, the usual. Stayin' late at work, comin' home with under-wear inside out, that sort of thing. I've seen it all before.

Every guy's got their place where they hang out with friends, watch the game, knock back a few beers, flirt with the bar-maid. She said it was The Haven, asked if I knew it. Sure, I knew it. I knew it well. That's where I met my man. He's per-fect, no wife, no kids. He's honest, somethin' you don't see every day, especially in this business. We were meetin' that night and then we'd go to my place, as usual.

She gave me a picture so's I could stake out the bar. It was one of those photo Christmas cards: three kids, cocker spaniel, picket fence. There he was, wearing the same shirt he had on when I first took him home.

Cher's Fat Lesbian Daughter

Antay Bilgutay

Play
Early 40s
Comic
Contemporary

Claire is the downstairs neighbor of Larry who has recently broken up with his partner and is listening to Cher's "Dark Lady." (It was their song.) Claire hears the music and, drunk, bursts into Larry's apartment.

Look, neighbor. I'm not gonna pour my heart out here. I don't know you. You don't know me. I'm Claire from downstairs. (. . .). And I needed to stop that horseshit music. (. . .) Listen: my girlfriend just left me for Chastity Bono. That's right. Chastity Bono. Cher's fat lesbian daughter. Fucking Cher. Fat Chastity. The bitch stole my girlfriend, and as a result I am drunk as Dean Martin at a keg party. They met at some stupid conference or something in D.C. Some fucking human rights convention. Well, what about *my* rights, Chastity? Chastity Bono just drags her wide celebrity ass over there and seduces her. I'm thinking, how can I compete? My mother doesn't have tattoos. My mother wasn't born in the wagon of a travelin' show. And as I'm pacing in the hallway, trying to sort shit out, I hear "Dark Lady" coming from upstairs. I thought: I am gonna kill the ironical bastard who's playing that. (. . .) I swear, at this instant, I just want Chastity Bono to blow up or die by my hands. And while I recognize that morally such an action would be wrong, frankly I don't give a rat's ass.

Circus Schism
Arthur Jolly

Play
45-55
Seriocomic
Contemporary

This professional dominatrix is strong, but tired.

I should've waited for a cab. I always catch a cab, but midday, midtown, and it's raining? That's three strikes, and you're out on the street in the rain. So I jumped on the R train, and some cow sees the boots and decides I'm her personal bitch-post for the day. And she just didn't get it. She's ranting, blaming me for the ills of womankind, centering around her perfect precious self and how she can't get a good man. Bitch, you don't deserve one. She's sitting there, and she's wearing high heels. And she's got nails out to here, and a dress too tight to walk in. What's her goddamn excuse? I'm wearing the same things, I push it a little, but that's my fucking job. She works in a goddamn office. She answers the telephone with an earpiece that plugs directly into her frontal lobe. And she just didn't get it. Heels and a tight skirt. And this bitch—she tells me, "You think you're empowered, the one in control—but you're not. You're being degraded for their pleasure."

Like she knew anything about me. Like she knew anything about power. I mean . . . what the fuck does she think? That I don't know that? You don't judge me. I know who's paying, I know who the customer is. (. . .)

What does she know about power? What do any of them know?

Conditional Commitment

Terese Pampellonne

Play
Late 30s
Dramatic
Contemporary

*Leslie is going to have an abortion, in spite of her boyfriend
wanting to keep it. In a Mexican restaurant, after a few cold
ones, she explains her reason to a dinner companion.*

Happy family? Hah (. . .) [W]hen I was little my father doted
on me. (. . .) I never saw my parents kiss once during their
entire marriage, but every day after work he'd come home, pick
me up and give me the biggest kiss. (. . .) Our carpeting was
worn so thin you could see the floorboards underneath but my
father always came up with the money to buy me the newest
Barbie. It used to piss my mother off. What about me? she'd
cry. Everything's for her! They used to fight all the time about it
until one day I came home from school early. My dad had been
laid off so they were arguing more than usual (. . .). I heard
my mother say she wanted a divorce and next thing I knew
Dad was tearing off down the street in the Pontiac. At the
time, I felt like it was my fault. (. . .) I just wanted to fix
things so bad. So I went upstairs and lined up every single
doll I had. There they were smiling their doll-smiles . . . it
should have made a mother proud. (. . .) Instead . . . they
made me angry. (. . .) I began to stomp on them . . . kick
them, rip their arms and legs out (. . .) until finally my mother
found me, crying, surrounded by all my dolls in various stages
of dismemberment. (*She laughs.*) (. . .)

She wasn't mad or anything. Instead, she screwed their heads back on and pressed their arms and legs back into their sockets. And then, in a voice as calm as bathwater, she said, "Gently, you must treat babies very gently, otherwise when you're asleep, they'll come into your bed and eat you alive."

Corn, Hogs, and Indians

Avanti A. Pradhan

Original Monologue
20+
Seriocomic
Contemporary

*A young woman reflects on what it was like to be raised as a
first-generation Indian-American girl in a mid-sized, white-
bread Middle American town.*

I grew up in Des Moines, Iowa. Land of corn, hogs, suburbs,
and . . . white people. As you might have guessed, Des Moines
wasn't exactly the Mecca of diversity when I was growing up. I
remember endless days of wishing that my skin was a little
more fair, and that my upper lip was a little less hairy. I remember having to constantly correct my mom's pronunciation of the
word *vegetable,* which she pronounced as "vez-e-table". And I
remember being embarrassed of my extremely well-educated
parents when a pimply-faced teenager taking drive-through
orders couldn't understand what they were saying. My mom
would order the same thing every time, a "vezetarian" burger.
And every time, it would be the same routine. The drive-
through boy would say, "A-aight, a veze-what?" . . . I would
slump down in the passenger seat trying to hide myself . . . and
Mommy would ask to speak to the manager. My mom always
had to speak with the manager. Why couldn't she have acted
like Becky's mom? I'm sure Becky never had this sort of problem with the drive-through boy. I'm sure Becky and her mom
drove in and out of the fast-food joint in a matter of minutes.
But, then again, if my mom can understand that "a-aight"
means "all right", then the drive-through boy *should* understand that "vezetarian" means "vegetarian" . . . A-aight?

Crimes of the Heart
Beth Henley

Play
20s
Dramatic
Contemporary

Babe had an affair with Willy Jay, a young black man. After watching her husband, Zachary, abuse Willy Jay, she shoots her husband. Here, she tells her sister what went through her head in those final moments.

After that, I don't remember too clearly; let's see? I went on into the living room, and I went right up to the davenport and opened the drawer where we keep the burglar gun? I took it out. Then I—I brought it up to my ear. That's right. I put it right inside my ear. Why I was gonna shoot off my own head! That's what I was gonna do. Then I heard the back door slamming and suddenly, for some reason, I thought about Mama? how she'd hung herself. And here I was about ready to shoot myself. Then I realized—that's right, I realized how I didn't want to kill myself! And she—she probably didn't want to kill herself. She wanted to kill him, and I wanted to kill him, too. I wanted to kill Zackery, not myself. 'Cause I—I wanted to live! So I waited for him to come on into the living room. Then I held out the gun, and I pulled the trigger, aiming for his heart but getting him in the stomach. *(Pause.)* It's funny that I really did that.

The Curious Incident of the Dog in the Night-Time

Mark Haddon

Novel
35+
Dramatic
Contemporary

In this letter, a mother of an autistic teen attempts to explain her absence.

I was not a very good mother, Christopher. Maybe if things had been different, maybe if you'd been different, I might have been better at it. But that's just the way things turned out.

I'm not like your father. Your father is a much more pacient person. (. . .) Do you remember once when we were shopping in town together? And we went into Bentalls and it was really crowded and we had to get a Christmas present for Grandma? And you were frightened because of all the people in the shop. It was the middle of Christmas shopping when everyone was in town. And I was talking to Mr. Land who works on the kitchen floor and went to school with me. And you crouched down on the floor and put your hands over your ears and you were in the way of everyone. So I got cross, because I don't like shopping at Christmas, either, and I told you to behave and I tried to pick you up and move you. But you shouted and you knocked those mixers off the shelf and there was a big crash. And everyone turned round to see what was going on. (. . .) And then I had to walk you all the way home which took hours because I knew you wouldn't go on the bus again. (. . .) Your father is really pacient but I'm not, I get cross, even though I don't mean too.

Currents

Roger Nieboer

Play
40+
Dramatic
Contemporary

The setting is post-apocalyptic. Bernice stands behind a cash register, hooked up to an I.V.

It happens in the back. Where I unpack the crates. If they're alive, I snap their wings so they can't fly out of the baskets. And·if they're already dead, I throw 'em in a pile over there for the guy who makes soup. He don't care. If they're dead or not. How they died. As long as there's some meat on the bones. He never says too much. He asks about my husband sometimes. Says he knew him in the war. And his hands are up inside my sweater. I don't mind exactly. They're warm. Very warm and one of the thumbs is missing. He's never too grabby or all rough and in a hurry like a young buck. He just holds me. He cups 'em there nice an' warm and slow 'til the tips rise up through his fingers. So he's got 'em there almost like a pliers, but he doesn't pinch. No, not the soup man. He holds me in his fingers, in his hands, in his arms. He holds me in and I feel like my whole body is gonna sneeze. And then we go back, not falling exactly cuz he's holding me and lifting my skirts. But we go back in a pile of feathers. Further and further back. And everything tightens. Everything feels very tight. And there's this sound, this grating sound grinding. He's grinding his teeth together and whispering goddammit. Goddammit not in the way it's usually said, but in a special way. All soft and gentle like an angel singing Chattanooga Choo-choo. And by the time we hit the floor, by the time our rubber boots get down to the concrete, I can see the lice. Jumping off the feathers up on our skin. I smell the blood and ammonia and dead birds. I get up . . . wash off the both of us with a warm rag . . . and I ask him . . . *(Pause.)* I ask him what the war was like and he says he doesn't wanna talk about it. And I go back to snappin' wings.

Curse of the Starving Class

Sam Shepard

Play
40+
Seriocomic
Contemporary

Ella counsels her daughter, Emma, who has started her period.

[But] I want you to know the truth. I want you to know all the facts before you go off and pick up a lot of lies. Now, the first thing is that you should never go swimming when that happens. It can cause you to bleed to death. The water draws it out of you. (. . .)

The next thing is sanitary napkins. You don't want to buy them out of any old machine in any old gas station bathroom. I know they say "sanitized" on the package but they're a far cry from "sanitized." They're filthy in fact. They've been sitting around in those places for months. You don't know whose quarters go into those machines. Those quarters carry germs. Those innocent looking silver quarters with Washington's head staring straight ahead. His handsome jaw jutting out. Spewing germs all over those napkins.

(. . .) They're not hospital clean that's for sure. And you should know that anything you stick up in there should be absolutely hospital clean.

A Day at the Beach
Beth Sager

Play
20s-30s
Dramatic
Contemporary

This woman's mother is an alcoholic. The daughter is looking at a picture taken several years ago while they were on the beach.

I look at this picture of the two of us on the beach, and despite the reflections of mother and daughter, all I can see is my anger. You were drinking. You couldn't go one afternoon without the liquor. There's no doubt in my mind what was more important to you. If you were forced to make the choice, there would have been none. If I had said it's either the booze, or me, I would be looking at just a picture of you. If someone saw this photograph they would say, what a nice family picture it was, what a happy moment. Captured for all to see. They would never realize there was a third party lurking in the shadow of the umbrella. They would never realize the secret behind your smile, or the pain behind mine. They would never know that the happy memory I should have had, was stolen by the very smile on your face. When I look at it, I don't see your face or the sun shining. I don't see the tide lapping in the background or the families playing. All I see is my anger. It burns hotter than the sun, and more predictable than the tide.

Dear Chuck

Jonathan Dorf

Play
Teen
Dramatic
Contemporary

A swim club. The actor perhaps holds a rubber ducky, a towel.
and whatever else would make her suitably dressed to go swim-
ming. The actor points at a lifeguard.

I should totally get a lawyer and sue that guy. (. . .)

Don't give me that look like you don't know what I'm
talkin' about. Playin' dumb isn't gonna' keep me out of the
kiddie pool. The sign doesn't even say "kiddie pool." It says
"wading pool." I want to wade. I'm real big on wading. I wade
at the beach. I wade in the pond near my house, even waded in
the Dead Sea once, which is really hard 'cause all the salt makes
you float. Who am I bothering if I wade here? I mean hey—I'm
probably the only person in there that wouldn't change the
color of the water.

(Pause.)

The lifeguard says maybe if there's nobody else in the pool
he'd let me swim. So I'm watchin'. The kids from the summer
camp are at the snack bar having their afternoon cookies and
bug juice, so they're all getting out. But just as the camp kids
are finally gone, there's this one little twerp—looks like he's
two, maybe three—got those elbow flotation things, and he's
crying his head off and his mom or nanny or housekeeper or
whatever is draggin' him in. He obviously doesn't want to go—
he's trying to bite her hand—so why doesn't this crazy lady just

give the kid some time to get over it and stop scarring him for life. Because I don't want to see him turn into a psychopathic killer, and I don't own a bathtub, so this way, everybody gets what they want.

(Pause.) (. . .)

I'm thinkin' about a petition. Or a boycott. Or maybe a march where everybody sings "We Shall Overcome." A lot. In a round. Because this is age discrimination, and it really sucks.

Distance
Grace Paley

Short Story
45+
Seriocomic
Contemporary

John has just announced to his parents that he plans to marry a neighbor girl, Virginia. His mother, who knows everything that goes on in their New York neighborhood, has something to say about her son's decision.

Then what of last Saturday night, you had to go to the show yourself as if there wasn't no one else in the Borough of Manhattan to take to a movie, and when you was gone I seen her buy two Cokes at Carlo's and head straight to the third floor to John Kameron's (. . .) and come out at 11 P.M. and his arm was around her. (. . .) . . . and his hand was well under her sweater.

It *is* so, and tell me, young man, how you'll feel married to a girl that every wild boy on the block has been leaning his thumbs on her titties like she was a Carvel dairy counter, tell me that? (. . .)

[Y]ou listen to me, Johnny Raftery, you're somebody's jackass, I'll tell you, you look out that front window and I bet you if you got yourself your dad's spyglass you would see some track of your little lady. I think there are evenings she don't get out of the back of that trailer truck parked over there and it's no trouble at all for Pete or Kameron's half-witted kid to get his way of her. Listen Johnny, there isn't a grown-up woman who was sitting on the stoop last Sunday when it was so damn windy that doesn't know that Ginny don't wear underpants.

Docent

R. T. Smith

Short Story
40s+
Comic
Contemporary

Miss Sibby conducts a tour of historic Lee Chapel.

Good Afternoon, ladies and gentlemen from hither and yon, and welcome to the Lee Chapel on the campus of historic Washington and Lee University. My name is Sybil Mildred Clemm Legrand Pascal, and I will be your guide and compass on this dull, dark, and soundless day, as the poet says, in the autumn of the year. You can call me Miss Sibby, and in case you are wondering about my hooped dress of ebony, my web-like hairnet and calf-leather shoes, they are authentic to the period just following the War Between the States, and I will be happy to discuss the cut and fabric of my mourning clothing with any of you fashion-conscious ladies at the end of the tour (. . .) No camera flashes, please, in the General Lee alcove. No smoking, of course—a habit I deplore. (. . .)

As we enter the vestibule, please do us the kindness of signing our guest register, which bears the autographs of presidents and princes, as well as luminaries from Reynolds Price to Burt Reynolds, from Maya Lin, the memorial designer, to Rosalynn Carter, Woodrow Wilson, Bing Crosby, Vincent Price, and the Dalai Lama. Fifty thousand visitors annually, I believe, many of them repeaters, from far and away, devotees of Lee, people who love the Stars and Bars or have a morbid curiosity, I suppose about the fall of the South. If you have a morbid curiosity about the fall of the South—which is not the same as a healthy historical interest—please save your comments for your own diaries and private conversations. One of my cardinal epigrams, a compilation of which I will pen myself someday under the title "Miss Sibby Says," is this: "History is not gossip; opinion is seldom truth."

The Doomsday Club

Terese Pampellonne

Play
30s
Comic
Contemporary

*Sheila's suit is wrinkled, her nylons are run, her French twist is
unraveling, and her thick lenses are sliding down her nose. She
is a walking fidget, constantly adjusting all of the above.*

Doctor Lang told me that under hypnosis I confessed that my
parents bowling league was just a cover for one of the
Midwest's largest Satanic cults of which . . . my father was the
leader! (. . .) After that, of course I became a therapy junkie.
I saw my doctor twice a day and was on the phone with her
weekends. Every dream was a new revelation, every revelation
brought new understanding. You wouldn't believe what a mind
can hide! But for the first time in my life I was . . . (*Blissful
smile.*) happy. (*Pause.*) At least, I thought I was. I mean, if
you're going to be addicted to something . . . it might as well be
self-discovery, right? (*Sigh.*) Except, it turned out my uncon-
scious wasn't trying to communicate with me at all. Dr. Lang
was arrested for insurance fraud. They said she was program-
ming all of her patients to believe they were cult victims.
There's a lot of money in it, you know, because victims of
satanic cults need therapy for at least the rest of their lives. And
as for my parents . . . they weren't Satanists at all. Just . . .
(*Brings a tissue to her eyes.*) really bad bowlers.

Drinking and Diving
David Epstein

Play
20s
Seriocomic
Contemporary

Daisy does a lousy job of talking down a jumper—who also happens to be a diver.

You, a guy with everything. Jesus. You talk about hypocrisy? Buddy, you don't even know what hypocrisy is. Your family must have dumped hundreds of thousands of dollars into your all-important little dream to be the number one diver in the world. Your problems are for shit, and boo hoo, your father recently died. So what? I don't even know who my father is! I met him once years ago, and he looked like a derelict anyway, and I don't even know if it was really him. Once! So boo-fucking-hoo. You've had experiences that most people can only dream of, and you take that for granted as if you're entitled to even more justice than you've already been given? My God. I wonder how I even made it this far without throwing myself in front of a bus for daring to think that my life was OK, because it's not. It's ridiculous. So go ahead. Do your thing. Jump. Jump away and I'll call down to the street sweepers and let them know you're on the way down. But one thing is for sure. The judges will give you deductions for having some splash. It won't be a perfect dive no matter how hard you try. It'll be the worst dive of your life, but I'm ready to watch you go. Hell.

Eloise & Ray

Stephanie Fleischmann

Play
16
Dramatic
Contemporary

Eloise, having lost her virginity to her boyfriend, basks in the aftermath.

I said to Rosanna. "Him and me, we— He devirginized me. Yesterday. I am now de." And she said, "Congratulations. From this moment on, in honor of this, I will call you DeVee."

And I said, "Not around my daddy, you won't."

"That's right," she said. "He would KILL you if he found out. But MY lips are zipped."

And then she looked at me and she looked at me for the longest time, and I said, (. . .) "Do I look different?"

And she said, "No. You look like Eloise. You look like you always did. Do you feel like her?"

"Her?" I said.

"Eloise," she said. "Same old same old."

"But the same old same old feels different every day," I said.
See-through.

"You know what I mean," she said.

And so I told her: "I do. I feel different."
Glow in the dark.

"I feel like I am his and he is mine and he will never leave me. He will never let me go. (. . .) I feel a changing— I am the me that was always meant to be. (. . .) I feel like an oyster. All this time I been an oyster, and I never even knew it. All this time takin' in sand and takin' in sand and it's been workin' on me, workin' inside me to make this— This pearl. Only it took him to pry me open and pick it out."

Erratica
Reina Hardy

Play
35-45
Comic
Contemporary

*Dr. Samantha Stafford is an English professor writing a book
on Shakespeare in the midst of several distractions—including a
student who is madly in love with her. She has just finished
reading his poem.*

Mr. Fairland . . . Gregory, isn't it? Uh-huh. Well, Gregory.
Before I go any further in my critique of this piece, I'd like to
inquire if I ever actually assigned a free-form, slant-rhymed,
revisionist sonnet in what seems suspiciously like praise to my
Renaissance Forms class? Really? I thought not. Though it did
sound like something I might do to buck myself up for a date.

Now, Gregory. If you'd hoped to seduce me with this you're out
of luck. (. . .) It's very, very bad. Laughable, actually. If you
really wanted me, you should have come in here and played
your strengths. Your ass, for instance. I noticed that it's tight,
toned, well-rounded and vigorous . . . which is a lot more than
I can say for your sonnet.

Listen, Gregory. You're not such a bad writer. (. . .) If you
want my respect, take it home, think about how you're using
the meter, put a corset on those rampant double entendres and
gut the third stanza. It's nothing but abstraction. If, however,

you just want to get laid, get rid of the teaching references and try it out on a freshman. *(Drops the papers on the far side of her desk, and retrieves her glasses.)*

Good day, Gregory.

Father's Day

Oliver Hailey

Play
35+
Comic
Contemporary

Men—can't live with them, can't kill them.

Well, suppose I get it out in the open. Dear old Tom and I got a divorce because we didn't really care for one another. In the seven wonderful years we were married, I struck him with brooms, mops, my electric curling iron—assorted feminine apparatus. He swung at me with golf clubs, a baseball bat, a walking stick—items of the male gender. I once tried to strangle him with my hair dryer cord. He tried it on me with his electric razor cord. When he was a little tight one night, I tried to force a swizzle stick down his throat. When he was sober enough, he tried that on me. I took that dangerous little plastic bag that comes from the dry cleaner's, tried my damnedest to hold it over his head. He then proceeded to have a suit cleaned—not an original bone in his body—and jumped me at the door one evening with his plastic bag. I tried to run him down with the car twice before he even figured out what I was doing. When he finally figured it out, he tried to run me down with it. In short, it wasn't a good marriage. We got a divorce because we really didn't dig one another. And I hope to God I am typical—and speak for most of the divorced people in the country—when I say that is why we get divorced.

Faye

Rob Matsushita

Play
Mid-teens
Comic
Contemporary

Faye leaves a message on Connie's answering machine.

It's me, pick up. I have to tell you something. If I must know, you must know.

You are so totally home. Pick up!

Connie, pick the fuck up!

Sorry, Connie's mom.

OK, I'll just tell you:

Franklin told me that he likes you.

Yeah!

OK, so, call Franklin.

Oh, wait.

You probably don't know Franklin's number.

I don't know it either.

OK.

Oh! Oh! I can totally go over to his house! I know where he lives, because of that time we followed him.

I go over, and I talk to him. And then I call you from there, and when you get home, you can call us.

OK?

Oh, but if you're doing Bake Sale duty today, you won't be home for a while.

Hmmm.

OK: New plan.

I go to his place, and invite him to my place. I can make him want to go.

Then you just call me back, and he'll be here!

And . . . I get him really, really drunk.

See, then he won't leave.

Three sips of 180 proof grain alcohol, you really can't get out of a bean bag chair.

So, that's the plan.

Connie's mom? If you were listening? This is all, like, a joke.

The Feast of Love

Charles Baxter

Novel
20s
Comic
Contemporary

Chloe, an employee at Jitters, a coffee shop in a mall, considers things carefully.

I can be *so* unmotivated. For example. You know the dust that can, like, float in the air? Me, I was totally capable of sitting in a chair for *hours,* watching the dust-fuzz hanging in front of me. If there was sunlight in the room, just the particles of visible molecules or whatever, I was excellent and enthralled.

I'm not saying that I'm deep, I'm just saying I watch the dust, and I'm not stoned either, when I do it. Just observant. I'm concentrating on it, figuring out its mystery, its purpose for being here in the same universe with us.

When I tried to get Oscar to study the dust, he went: you're so, like, Looney Tunes, Chloé. Jeez, dust. He *was* smiling when he said that, criticizing my dust interest. But you could tell that he didn't get the profundity of dust at all. Poor guy. Well, some people can't sing, either.

The Fish Bowl

Jocelyn Hughes

Original Monologue
20s-30s
Comic
Contemporary

Lisa, a Hollywood executive from Hell, shares her candid opinion of Bobby's screenplay.

So, I've read your screenplay and I think it sucks. (. . .)

Yeah, your dialogue is just atrocious, your characters have absolutely no arc and obviously plot is a little too sophisticated for you. You've heard of conflict resolution before, right?(. . .) Tell me again why you decided to become a screenwriter? Wait, don't tell me, you were fat, unattractive and your best friends were Strunk and White? No, just joking . . . you're pretty thin. (. . .)

I was also joking about the Strunk and White part. In case you don't know, they were writing partners for the majority of grammar books you read in high school. I realize that joke may be a little (*Using her hands to indicate air quotes.*) "highbrow" for you. You've heard of that phrase before, right? Now that we're cooking with gas, a writing partner may not be such a bad idea for you. I'll give Allen Ball a call and ask him to write something that you can put your name on . . . not! Goodness.

(Awkward pause.)

(Overly friendly.) So, how are you?

Freshwater: A Comedy

Virginia Woolf

Play
40+
Seriocomic
Contemporary

A woman finds the policemen at Freshwater lacking in certain musculature.

What is the use of a policeman if he has no calves? There you have the tragedy of my life. That is Julia Margaret Cameron's message to her age! All my sisters were beautiful, but I had genius. They were the brides of men, but I am the bride of Art. I have sought the beautiful in the most unlikely places. I have searched the police force at Freshwater, and not a man have I found with calves worthy of Sir Galahad. But, as I said to the Chief Constable, "Without beauty, constable, what is order? Without life, what is law?" Why should I continue to have my silver protected by a race of men whose legs are aesthetically abhorrent to me? If a burglar came and he was beautiful, I should say to him: Take my fish knives! Take my cruets, my breadbaskets and my soup tureens. What you take is nothing to what you give, your calves, your beautiful calves.

Fur

Migdalia Cruz

Play
30s
Comic
Contemporary

Nena is an animal trapper who worships Michael, the hand-some owner of Joe's Pet Shop.

He's like God to me . . . well, maybe not God, himself—
I mean, really I'm not sure I believe in one person like that. I
mean, really, too many friends have died for me to believe
that—really. But he's a person surrounded by white light . . .
Not like a clown or a mime—I mean, I hate mimes—but he's a
different kind of white . . . like light, I mean. And I don't just
mean the clothes. He wears white, of course, and so few people
can, I mean and do it well—but he's light on the inside. I think
it's because he cares about animals so much. And I attract
animals—without traps or mechanical snares—I just look at
them and they're mine . . . And I give them to him—I would do
it for free except I don't think he'd respect me for that. So I put
a price on it, and he appreciates that . . . I think. I think with a
price he's assured of their value. Nothing wrong with that—I
don't think . . . I think I love him.

Give It Up
Norman A. Bert

Original Monologue
20s
Seriocomic
Contemporary

Margo, a prostitute, has offered Joe money to help him while he's out of work. He turns it down, but tells Margo that he loves her. Margo responds.

Who do you think you are? Jesus? Well, go find another cross to die on. I ain't available. (*She gathers her thoughts.*) Sorry, but religion's a crock. Nobody walks on water. How can a smart guy like you believe stories about some dead guy showin' up like a spook at a party? Levitating Jesus. (*Snorts a laugh.*) And then drinking blood and eating the body? Gross. I gave it a shot, too—don't think I didn't. Went to church camp when I was thirteen. My mom thought it'd help get me on the right track. 'Course she didn't know about Preston. Good ol' Preston. Camp counselor. Real Christian. Real horny. Took a real *interest* in li'l Margo, ol' Preston did. But all that aside, what really burns me about religion? You. You thinkin' that just 'cause *you're* ruining *your* life, *I* oughta reform. What a crock. (*To JOE.*) Give it up, Jesus.

Goodnight Desdemona (Good Morning Juliet)

Ann-Marie MacDonald

Play
Mid-20s
Seriocomic
Contemporary

Constance has just been dumped, screwed out of a position at Oxford, and told she is to take a teaching position at an isolated college on the Canadian prairie.

Regina. I hate the prairies. They're flat. It's an absolute nightmare landscape of absolutes and I'm a relativist. I'll go mad. (. . .) I can't feel anything. I'm perfectly fine. I'll call the Dean and resign. I'll go back to my apartment and watch the plants die and the cats copulate freely. I'll order in groceries. Eventually I'll be evicted. I'll smell really bad and swear at people on the subway. Five years later I run into Professor Night and Roman: they don't recognize me. I'm selling pencils. They buy one. Suddenly, I drop dead. They discover my true identity. I'm awarded a doctorate posthumously. Professor Night dedicates his complete works to me and lays roses on my grave every day. My stone bears a simple epithet: "Oh what a noble mind is here o'erthrown." (. . .) There's no time to lose! I have to start right now if I'm going to sink that low in five years.

Handler

Robert Schenkkan

Play
45-55
Dramatic
Contemporary

Terri lives in the rural south. She is tending a grave.

I get over when I can and pull them weeds. Usta come all the time but they always grow back. Even when I dig 'em out by the roots. Sister Alice said I ought to use weed killer but that don't seem right, somehow. Poison. Don't know why it should matter but it does. And sometimes I bring flowers. We get to keep what we find in the rooms we clean, long as it ain't real valuable. (. . .) You find some strange things, I tell you what. (. . .)

Anyways, sometimes, people order flowers up to their rooms. Anniversaries and suchlike, I guess. Special occasions. I don't know why they leave'm. I wouldn't. I mean, even if you didn't want to carry 'em back wet in the car, you could always dry 'em, you know? Or press 'em inna book. Keepsakes. Remembrance. Some people set up vases of plastic flowers out here but that always seems so tacky to me. Plastic. Be puttin' up pink flamingos and daisy wheels next. Gravel's the new thing. White, shiny gravel. Can you believe that? Dump it by the truckload. Cain't nothin' push up through that, believe you me. And if your . . . your dearly departed looks like a garden path or the bottom of a fish tank, well, that's just too bad, inn't? Me, I'd rather pull them weeds on my hands and knees.

(TERRI falls to the ground and begins yanking fiercely at the weeds.)

Hate Mail

Kira Obolensky and Bill Corbett

Play
20s-30s
Dramatic
Contemporary

Dahlia, a photographer, grapples with those who hate her work, and one man who, perhaps, loves it more than he should.

Hello, or should I say What the Hell?!

I write to ask you a question, not to resurrect the sputtering dialogue of months ago. Some background information: my exhibition was not the hoped-for critical success. Apparently, depicting the unclothed female body amid the urban pastoral of the twentieth century is more "suited to a Calvin Klein ad." (This from one of my ex-lovers, who I have discovered is just another snob underneath all that Comme des Garçons.) My circle of pseudofeministintellectual "friends" have accused me of creating "pornography that objectifies the female form for male/capitalist consumption." Exactly! . . . I would say, if for one second I was given the opportunity to defend myself. It's political, you morons! The body depicted is my own: the artist's body, displayed, revealed, to be tragically consumed by market forces as a tourist might covet a trinket.

Which brings me to my main point. Despite the overwhelmingly negative response, every single photograph in the exhibition has been purchased. The gallery dealer will tell me only that the anonymous collector is "a gentleman from the Midwest."

The idea that you might own twelve photographs of my naked body is very alarming to me. Did you purchase my photographs? And if you did (a thought that makes every hair on my body stand at attention), WHY?

Have Mercy
Hope McIntyre

Play
15
Dramatic
Contemporary

1909. Louise is a runaway. Her mother has just been arrested for murdering the babies that were products of her husband's incestuous relationships with his daughters. The Women's League, which is working in her mother's defense, has asked Louise for her testimony.

He was a stuffed, hairy pig. All pink and fat. When he got angry he'd turn bright red like a cherry. He was always "the man" because I had no love for him. None of us did. I was fifth of ten. I mostly stayed invisible. I was scared of him, sure. When I was nine he tried to touch me and I took a pitchfork and stuck him like the stuffed pig that he is. I knew he'd try to kill me after that, so I run off. Never went back, never want to go back neither. There's too much blackness there and I don't think that'll ever change even with him in prison. Everyone thought he was some evil force, stronger than anything, unstoppable. But, he's a fat old man and he's mortal. Now, the babies, well it's too bad about them. What would you do if you thought you'd given birth to the devil's spawn? Nancy never thought of them as babies. My mother figured that it was the least she could do for her. That's what happens when you feel you've got no options. I'd seen enough.

Herbert III

Ted Shine

Play
Late 30s
Seriocomic
Contemporary

Margarette is a loving mother, protective of her sons. After sending her husband Herbert out to look for their son, Herbert the Third, she calls her mother.

Mama? This is Margarette . . . No, we're alright . . . Yes'm, Herbert's alright . . . No'm, we ain't got no death, Mama. I called because . . . well . . . Herbert the Third ain't home, and it's almost four! . . . I donno where he went to, Mama . . . I *know* he's not at your place. Herbert went to look for him . . . Mama, I *know* you have to be at work in the mornin', but he's your grandson too! Ain't you worried? . . . I just tol'you it's nearly four and he's not in this house! . . . He could be dead for all I know! . . . Mama, I have insurance on *all* my family! . . . Yes, the premiums're paid! You talk like you *hope* somethin' mighta happened to your grandchild! . . . I know you don't want nothin' to happen, Mama, neither do I . . . I can't sleep . . . I know you was asleep, Mama, but this is important to me. Mama! Mama, don't hang up!

Horrible Child

Lawrence Krauser

Play
Preteen
Dramatic
Contemporary

Horrible, a child, is horrible.

An arm's length for you, for me ten thousand yards—
I see there ten cards, I got five. I live
like a maggot off your ill-processed feast;
to my yeast rise your flour, to the west set the hour;
no time. So flow the sources of my remorses.
So what, I'm Horrible, leave me alone.
Go smother your gardens, scratch your horizons
Go grow beneath you brambles of cobras
I'm Horrible and that's what is,
that sums up the dumb nut of your oafish ravings
the depleted savings of your rusted tabernacle;
I'm Horrible and it ain't gonna change.
I'm Horrible as they come and I come harder,
I'm Horrible as I come and as they goes,
I'm Horrible as I come and as I doze,
Horrible—*c'est moi*; Horrible—*autre fois*;
I'm Horrible as It gets 'cause I am It;
Why don't you run?

House Hunting

Henry W. Kimmel

Play
55
Seriocomic
Contemporary

A married couple is deciding whether to buy a house in which a gruesome murder once took place. As they survey the house, they meet up with Audrey Shur who, though she may be imagined, gives Jan insight about how a seemingly good marriage can fall apart.

When you're young and in love, you think nothing about sharing a twin bed. Two people cramped together, arm in arm. There's nowhere to move, but you don't care—you're in love. Then you get married and you move to a Queen. More room, less contact. Say good night and roll over. Kid wakes up in the middle of the night. No problem. Plenty of room in between. And pillows. Lots of pillows. Soft pillows. Hard pillows. Pillows just to take up space. Then you have more kids and you need a place to put all those pillows. So you work your way up to a King. Fall asleep and not even know the other person is there. Roll over twice just to say good night. Room for three kids in between. The spark dies, and it's all down hill. Pretty fast, in some cases. Finally, as the kids get older, the king is not enough. You thrash, he snores. Both of you talk in your sleep. So you get separate beds—twins—on opposite sides of the room. Need an appointment for sex. Which isn't bad because you're still at least thinking about it. Because the day comes when it's separate beds in separate rooms, and you leave the world pretty much the same way as you came in.

The House of Yes
Wendy MacLeod

Play
45+
Comedy
Contemporary

The House of Yes is the story of a dysfunctional family, the Pascals, who live across the street from the Kennedys in a wealthy suburb of Washington D.C. Mrs. Pascal has three children—a set of twins, Marty and Jackie (called Jackie-O because of her fixation on Jackie Kennedy) and a son, Anthony. Jackie-O is obsessed with assassinations and has only recently been released from a mental institution. The twins have had an incestuous relationship, and Jackie-O is in love with Marty. It is Thanksgiving Day and Marty has brought home a dinner guest—his fiancé, Lesly. Mom reacts.

Now don't get snippy with me Marty. You've been in this house less than thirty-seven seconds and you're already snippy. It's no wonder your father died young—he'd simply had it with all the snippiness. A person can die a slow death from being snipped at year after year. The way he said "solid" when he meant "salad" and the two of you would not let it go—like a puppy with a rag doll. Or the time he missed the exit on interstate 495. Those things *happen* on interstates, mistakes are made, that's what those No U Turn places are for. Now, let's stick to the subject:

Your sister has been out of the hospital less than six months. Last week she nearly lost it because the seltzer water was flat, and you bring a woman home. Not just a woman. A fiancée. An Anti-Jackie. Are you trying to push your sister over the edge? If Jackie were merely "ill" as you say, I could give her an aspirin and put her to bed—I could make her that soup you're supposed to make . . . chicken noodle . . . but alas I cannot. I mean I can make the soup for heaven's sake—it comes in a can—but I cannot make her well. I have tried—but to no avail. If there's anyone present who knows why this marriage should not take place, it is me.

Excuse me. I'm going to go baste the turkey and hide the sharp objects.

How I Learned to Drive
Paula Vogel

Play
16
Comic
Contemporary

Having just been belittled by her grandfather for her interest in Shakespeare, Lil' Bit jumps to her feet and gets the last word. Note: Although the character age here is sixteen, the actor must play Lil' Bit as an adult elsewhere in the play. Therefore, it is likely an older actor is playing sixteen.

You're getting old, Big Papa. You are going to die—very very soon. Maybe even *tonight*. And when you get to heaven, God's going to be a beautiful black woman in a long white robe. She's gonna look at your chart and say: Uh-oh. Fornication. Dog-ugly mean with blood relatives. Oh. Uh-oh. Voted for George Wallace. Well, one last chance: If you can name the play, all will be forgiven. And then she'll quote, "The quality of mercy is not strained." Your answer? Oh, too bad—*Merchant of Venice*: Act IV, Scene iii. And then she'll send your ass to fry in hell with all the other crackers. Excuse me, please.

How I Learned to Drive
Paula Vogel

Play
35+
Comic
Contemporary

Mother delivers to daughter Lil' Bit tips on drinking alcohol in the company of men.

Thanks to judicious planning and several trips to the ladies' loo, your mother once out-drank an entire regiment of British officers on a good-will visit to Washington! Every last man of them. Milquetoasts! How'd they ever kick Hitler's cahones, huh? No match for an American lady—I could drink every man in here under the table. *(Delivers one last crucial hint before she is gently "bounced.")* As a last resort, when going out for an evening on the town, be sure to wear a skin-tight girdle—so tight than only a surgical knife or acetylene torch can get it off you—so that if you do pass out in the arms of your escort, he'll end up with rubber burns on his fingers before he can steal your virtue—

The Hummingbird Play
Leslie Bramm

Original Monologue
30s-40s
Dramatic
Contemporary

Anna Rufous speaks the unspeakable.

Eighteen hours! That's how long my son fought to stay alive. That's how long he lay twisted and broken. That fragile body mangled, burnt! (. . .) Nobody was there to hold his hand. Thousands of miles from home, where was his mother? Someone rings the doorbell. Just like before. A General and three men in suits. I know who it is. Wives and mothers always know. I know as soon as the bell rings. I don't want to answer. I don't want to be home. They just keep ringing. You let them in. You open the door and let them in and now my son is dead. "We regret to inform you?" I say. "You must be mistaken. There must be some kind of mistake." The General has dry spit in the corner of his mouth. It looks like Tom's toothpaste. I catch the taste of fennel on my breath. He says my son's name. I think he's talking about you at first. I'm relieved. Then he repeats it, to make sure I hear. My son's death, simple as ringing a bell. Gritty and sweet, like the taste of toothpaste. (. . .) After a while I don't even hear the words. I watch his mouth. I watch the spit. I watch him trying to wet his lips.

They gave me a flag. Neatly folded . . . I gave them a man. A perfectly beautiful boy . . . He burned to death . . . I gave them a boy. They gave me a flag.

Hunter!
Nuba-Harold Stuart

Play
30s
Dramatic
Contemporary

Jerri explains to her new boyfriend, Jake, her style of loving.

I ain' no young girl . . . I done lived wid' a man befo'! . . . Fo'
six an' a' half years I lived wid' him! . . . An' he was a man! He
struggled, scuffled, an' went wid' out 'til he built this house for
us—brick by brick! (. . .) An' after he built it . . . he had 'da
nerve to call it "Our House!" Only thing is . . . I went out an'
picked 'da curtains fo' "Our House"—picked da dinette set . . .
'da "his and Her" towels . . . 'da sofa . . . 'da rug . . . I even
picked out his lounge chair! . . . All wid' out him! But it didn't
matter . . . to him it was still "Our House!" . . . 'Til . . . after
awhile . . . he began not ta' be able ta' find things in "Our
House." . . . Lil' things —like . . . keys! He was always
askin' . . . "Baby . . . where are m' keys?" . . . or . . .
"Baby . . . where are m' T-shirts?" (. . .) Befo' he even knew
what hit him—our house turned to "My House!" Just like
dat . . . he was a stranger in his own house . . . so he left! . . .
An' even tho' it took me a long time . . . now I know why he
had ta' leave ! (. . .) You gotta' understand 'dat sometimes you
love a person so hard . . . you just want to "DO!" . . . You
haveta' "DO!" An' sometime you do so much—you don't even
give 'da person you love a chance to "DO" fo' 'deyself! . . . I
can't help it! I was made to love somebody—to "DO" fo'
somebody! . . . Hunter's daddy useta' call it . . . "GO-rilla
Love!" An' I guess 'dat's just what it is—"GO-rilla Love!" . . .
An' Jake . . . if you don't think you strong enough to handle
it—you might as well leave.

Hurlyburly
David Rabe

Play
30s
Dramatic
Contemporary

During this monologue, Bonnie, a hacked-off exotic dancer, gets dressed.

I am a form of human being just like any other, get it! And you wanna try holding onto things on the basis of your fingernails, give me a call. So desperation, believe it or not, is within my areas of expertise, you understand? I am a person whose entire life with a child to support depends on her tits and this balloon and the capabilities of her physical grace and imaginary inventiveness with which I can appear to express something of interest in the air by my movement and places in the air I put the balloon along with my body, which some other dumb bitch would be unable to imagine or would fall down in the process of attempting to perform in front of crowds of totally incomprehensible and terrifying bunch of audience members. And without my work, what am I but an unemployed scrunt on the meat market of these streets? Because this town is nothin' but mean in spite of the palm trees. So that's my point about desperation, and I can give you references, just in case you never thought of it, you know; and just thought I was over here—some mindless twat over here with blonde hair and big eyes.

I Am What I Am

Aurora Levin Morales and Rosario Morales

Essay
25+
Dramatic
Contemporary

A proud assertion of heritage and cultural identity.

I am what I am and I am U.S. American I haven't wanted to
say it because if I did you'd take away the Puerto Rican but
now I say go to hell   I am what I am and you can't take it
away with all the words and sneers at your command   I am
what I am   I am Puerto Rican   I am U.S. American   I am
New York Manhattan and the Bronx   I am what I am I'm not
hiding under no stoop   behind no curtain I am what I am   I
am Boricua as boricuas come from the isle of Manhattan and I
croon Carlos Gardel tangoes in my sleep and Afro-Cuban beats
in my blood and Xavier Cugat's lukewarm latin is so familiar
and dear   sneer dear but he's familiar and dear   but not
Carmen Miranda   who's a joke because I never was a joke . . .
. . . I was a bit of a sensation   See! here's a real true honest-to-
god Puerto Rican girl and she's in college   Hey! Mary   come
here and look she's from right here a South Bronx girl and
she's honest-to-god in college now   Ain't that something   who
would believed it Ain't science wonderful or some such thing a
wonder a wonder

If You Went Missing

Kelly DuMar

Play
35-45
Seriocomic
Contemporary

Cin, a recently divorced mother, explains something basic to her thirteen year-old daughter.

I need to know where you're going after the game! *Why?* I'm glad you asked! Because I am your mother. That person in your life, who, beyond everyone else, and beyond reason or limit, *cares* about where you are going. I care because it is in my blood and bones to care. I care because whether or not you're satisfied with the result, I brought you kicking and screaming into this world. And, because I care, more than any other human being has, or will ever, care about you while you are traipsing over this earth, I need to know where you *are*. Because, if you went missing, by choice or by force, however small that horrible possibility may be, *I* would be compelled to *find* you. If I had to lose my job, become homeless and, snow-shoe across Siberia in a blizzard, I wouldn't stop searching until I *had* found you. Now, you may decide, much later in life, when you can no longer afford to avoid therapy, whether this kind of caring is loving devotion or bizarre fanaticism. But, like it or not, I'm on your trail. For life. So, I just need to know where you're going. Before you get there.

Imagine This
Alexander Speer

Original Monologue
Teens-20s
Dramatic
Contemporary

Darlene sits in a wheelchair. She can barely move her head.

Do you dream? I do. I don't know why. I'm sure it's not good for you. Dreaming is serious fun. People will tell you that's unhealthy. That's why I stay away from people. Dreaming pulls you out and up and away. I've been some really nice places in my dreams. Mars is my favorite. I don't much care for Martians, though. They don't like football. I don't trust people like that—even though they aren't people. They should still admire football. Some things are just basic. Mud wrestling is next. But you can't expect your typical Martian to understand something like that. Only the smartest understand mud wrestling. I always feel smart. But mostly I keep that a secret. I'm only telling you because you seem smart, too. You might even understand why I dream. I hope so. But I doubt it. A good dreamer needs a good reason. Most people don't have one. I do. That's why I feel so sad for you. If you could only be like me. I'm the happiest girl in the world. I travel up, up and away—and never leave the ground. Come fly with me. Up, up and away. We'll fly all the way to the stars.

In a Grove

Ryunosuke Akutagawa
Translated by Takashi Kojima

Short Story
20s+
Dramatic
Contemporary

Having been violated in the presence of her bound husband, a wife sees death as the only solution to their shared shame.

That man in the blue silk kimono, after forcing me to yield to him, laughed mockingly as he looked at my bound husband. How horrified my husband must have been! (. . .)

In the course of time I came to, and found that the man in the blue silk was gone. I saw only my husband still bound to the root of the cedar. I raised myself from the bamboo-blades with difficulty, and looked into his face. (. . .) Beneath the cold contempt in his eyes, there was hatred. Shame, grief, and anger . . . I didn't know how to express my heart at that time. (. . .)

"Takejiro," I said to him, "since things have come to this pass, I cannot live with you. I'm determined to die . . . but you must die, too. You saw my shame. I can't leave you alive as you are.

This was all I could say. Still he went on gazing at me with loathing and contempt. My heart breaking, I looked for his sword. Neither his sword nor his bow and arrows were to be seen in the grove. But fortunately my small sword was lying at my feet. Raising it overhead, once more I said, "Now give me your life. I'll follow you right away."

When he heard these words, he moved his lips with difficulty. Since his mouth was stuffed with leaves, of course his voice could not be heard at all. But at a glance I understood his words. Depising me, his look said only, "Kill me."

Keely and Du
Jane Martin

Play
25-30
Dramatic
Contemporary

Keely, raped and pregnant by her ex-husband, confides in Du, a member of an underground anti-abortion group who has kid-napped her.

I haven't ever been alone! Sharing with my brothers, moving in with roommates, moving in with Cole, moving back to Dad's, always other people in the room, always hearing other people talk, other people cough, other people sleep. Jesus! I dream about Antarctica, you know, no people, just ice. Nobody on your side of the bed, no do this, don't do that, no guys and what they want, what they have to have, just this flat, white, right, as far, you know, as far as you could see, like right out to the edge, no items, no chair, no cars, no people, and you can listen as hard as you want and you couldn't hear one goddamn thing.

Ladyhouse Blues

Kevin O'Morrison

Play
13
Seriocomic
Contemporary

Summer, 1919. St. Louis. Eylie talks to her older sister, who is about to be married.

Can I ask you somethin' else? (*Again without waiting.*) Havin' to become a Catholic so's you can marry Heinz Otto next month, an' all—how do you—*feel?*—(*To cover sudden embarrassment.*)—With his family being so *differn't.* (*Sees sister's hurt reaction*) Oh, Sis—I didn't mean to upset you. I just meant, why, I'll bet with a man as handsome as Heinz Otto you'd have agreed to become just about any old kind of religion. (*Beat.*) Which is kinda why it just came to me—all us Madden girls never had any real religion. I mean, growin' up on the farm, we learned the Bible—I can still recite all the Books, clear to Revelation—but we *weren't* anything. So when George asked Dot to become his religion, or Heinz Otto asks you—or if somebody *I* marry someday is something, I got no real reason not to become what he is, have I? (*Having arrived at the point of her recitation, she eyes her sister shyly.*) So when you went to Heinz Otto's priest for instruction—did you just learn a bunch of stuff, or were you—*changed?* (*Beat.*) 'Cause if'n you weren't, I don't hardly see the point of it.

Learning Curves
Allyson Currin

Play
Mid-20s
Seriocomic
Contemporary

Emma, who hears Shakespearean characters talking to her, is drunk, angry, and ready to seduce her undergraduate student, Jay.

You're done talking! All men are done talking until I am through!

And I know you hate it when I do this, but I'll be frank.

I'm not above sucking up to some sixty-year-old bull dyke if she's influential in the department. I've always made it a habit to sleep with the smartest men in my discipline. Because if the faculty pays attention to him, they'll pay attention to you.

It's a game. So, yes, I use the system.

But you're right about me being a subversive, too.

I'm a subversive and a sponge at the same time.

I'm a subversive sponge.

I play all the games I have to play. I flirt with the chair at the cocktail parties and suck up at the cookouts and wear tight shorts at the softball games against the history department.

It gets you noticed. And when you're noticed, people marvel that you don't just have a good ass, but you're smart too.

That gets you plumb assignments and good thesis committees.

It's a philosophy that's never failed me.

'Course I never had to flirt with such a cross old bitch in

my life—not to mention that castrated little weasel who drinks her bathwater—so now my whole philosophy has come back to bite me on my cute little ass!

So. System screws me. I screw System.

Do you have any idea what that means for you?

Fasten your seat belt, junior.

A Lesbian Appetite

Dorothy Allison

Short Story
30s+
Seriocomic
Contemporary

A self-titled "poor white-trash" woman explains that food is more than sustenance.

Red beans and rice, chicken necks and dumplings, pot roast with vinegar and cloves stuck in the onions, salmon patties with white sauce, refried beans on warm tortillas, sweet duck with scallions and pancakes, lamb cooked with olive oil and lemon slices, pan-fried pork chops and red-eye gravy, potato pancakes with applesauce, polenta with spaghetti sauce floating on top— food is more than sustenance; it is history. I remember women by what we ate together, what they dug out of the freezer after we'd made love for hours. I've only had one lover who didn't want to eat at all. We didn't last long. The sex was good, but I couldn't think what to do with her when the sex was finished. We drank spring water together and fought a lot.

Lesbians Who Kill

Peggy Shaw, Deborah Margolin, Lois Weaver

Play
Late 20s-40s
Seriocomic
Contemporary

May is being questioned about a series of murders on the Florida Interstate, men who had picked up a prostitute. This play is roughly based upon the Aileen Wuornos case.

There was a string of them? Not just one? Oh. Oh. On the highway? Ah. Is that what you wanted to talk to me about? Oh. The highway. Unh hunh. Yes, the highway. I love the highway. Oh, the Interstate? Unh hunh. You meet the most interesting people on the Interstate. Unh hunh. I love the Interstate. It leads to all parts of the body of the world! When I'm on the highway I feel like iron in someone's blood. (. . .)

Ah, the Interstate. The Florida Interstate. The names of people? The men's names? Dead men's names? I don't know. Open the newspaper, there's a million men's names in there. Let's pick some out! Millions of men. They're everywhere. In the phone book, the Bible, the sports page, the *Who's Who*, the Congress, the Senate, the *Daily News*!

Yes, I did. I know I did. I said I have something to confess, and I do. Lots of things. Like about my hair. Does it look OK? I tried a new hot oil treatment. It said on the box that it surrounds the hair at the shaft and coats it, shoots it full of new life. Is it true? Do you think it worked? Does my hair look surrounded, shot full of life? Like a stolen car on the Interstate! Ha! Funny how one thing resembles another! I always found that funny!

No, I don't hate men, how could I?

LGA-ORD

Ian Frazier

Essay
20s-30s
Comic
Contemporary

This is your captain speaking.

Extinguish the light extinguish the light I have extinguished the No Smoking light so you are free to move about the cabin have a good cry hang yourselves get an erection who knows however we do ask that while you're in your seats you keep your belts lightly fastened in case we encounter any choppy air or the end we've prayed for past time remembering our flying time from New York to Chicago is two hours and fifteen minutes the time of the dark journey of our existence is not revealed, you cry no you pray for a flight attendant you pray for a flight attendant a flight attendant comes now cry with reading material if you care to purchase a cocktail.

A cocktail?

If you care to purchase a piece of carrot, a stinking turnip, a bit of grit our flight attendants will be along to see that you know how to move out of this airplane fast and use seat lower back cushion for flotation those of you on the right side of the aircraft ought to be able to see New York's Finger Lakes region that's Lake Canandaigua closest to us those of you on the left side of the aircraft will only see the vastness of eternal emptiness without end. (. . .)

When we deplane I'll weep for happiness.

Liar

Brian Drader

Play
Mid-30s
Dramatic
Contemporary

*At the reception following her brother's funeral, Sherri meets a
drifter posing as her dead brother's lover.*

I'm glad you could come. There aren't many people here. I
didn't know who to call. I didn't know any of his friends. Was
he gay?

I'm sorry. That's none of my business. Well, of course it is. I'm
his sister. Of course it's my business. And I know he was. I
know that. And I'm not saying he was gay because he was a
nurse. I'm not stereotyping. There are plenty of straight nurses.
Aren't there? Anyway, that didn't make him gay. I know that.
I'm pretty sure that's why I never saw much of him, after . . .
after Mom and Dad died. I think he thought I wouldn't understand or something stupid like that. I would have. I would have
understood. I should have just called him up and asked him.
But you know how these things go, a year passes, two years,
five years, and before you know it, there's a hundred things
keeping you apart, all the bricks make a wall, and it's too high
to jump over and too thick to yell through, so you just let it go.
We had our own lives. Other things happened . . .

Can I freshen up your coffee? I'll get some more coffee. *(Begins
to leave, stops.)* Thanks. For coming. I appreciate it.

Lily Dale

Horton Foote

Play
18
Dramatic
Contemporary

Lily Dale, an emotional, self-involved Southern Belle has scolded her brother, Horace, for saying true, but hurtful things about their father, an alcoholic. In the midst of their argument, Horace collapses.

Oh, Brother. Brother! I'm sorry! Oh, dear Brother! I'm so sorry! I didn't mean a word of those terrible things I said. Not a one. I don't know what gets into me. I have a terrible disposition, Brother, a terrible disposition. It's the Robedaux coming out of me. Forgive me, please, please forgive me. *(She and HORACE are crying.)* I loved Papa. Believe me, I did. Just as much as you did. I loved him, but it hurts me so to talk about him, Brother. And it scares me, too. You don't know how it scares me. I wake sometimes in the night, and I think I can hear Papa coughing and struggling to breathe like he used to . . . and I didn't mean that about you leaving, Brother. I'm glad you're here and I want you to stay until you're all well and strong again. Because you're the only brother I have and sometimes at night, I see you dead and in your coffin and I cry in my dreams like my heart will break. I am really crying because my crying wakes me up and I say to myself, "Brother is alive and not dead at all, that's just a dream," but still I feel so miserable, I just lie there sobbing, like my heart will break. And sometimes Mama hears me and comes in and says, "Why are you crying, Lily Dale?" And I say, "Because I dreamt again that Brother was dead and had gone to heaven and left us." You're all the family I have, Brother, you and Mama. And we must never leave each other. Promise me you'll never leave me and promise me you'll forgive me. Promise me, promise me . . .

Listening
Edward Albee

Play
20+
Dramatic
Contemporary

The "acerbic and bitter" woman in Albee's three-person play shares a life-shaping event.

He was over seventy, my grandfather, and I think they'd been happy—though it was a generation wouldn't let you know, you know?—and one fine day he simply disappeared, didn't pack a bag, or act funny beforehand, simply said he was going into town to get some snuff, my grandmother used to tell him—snuff, for God's sake—and off he went, and do you think he came back? He did not! Never came back . . . the man at the tobacco store where they sold snuff said no, he'd not come in, when they asked, and you can be sure they did; and one man said he's seen him take a left at the library, and the policeman said no he'd seen him go off down Willow past the hardware store and Mrs. Remsen—the Lord rest her soul—said that wasn't true at all, that he said good day to her on the corner of Pocket and Dunder and sauntered off in the direction of the bank—to which, of course, it turned out he had not been. And so my grandmother made a map—being that way, you know: a methodical family—and found the locus where they all had seen him, some others, too, and determined from that, from all the information they'd put together, that from that spot, that locus, he had gone off in several directions at the same time. He had, in effect, dispersed.

Lizabeth: The Caterpillar Story

John Edgar Wideman

Short Story
30+
Seriocomic
Contemporary

*From inside the house, Lizabeth's mother comments as they
watch Daddy come home.*

Look at that man. You know where he been at. You know
what he's been doing. Look at him with his big hat self. You
know he been down on his knees at Rosemary's shooting crap
with them trifiling niggers. Don't you pay me no mind, child.
He's your daddy and a good man so don't pay me no mind if I
say I wish I could sneak out there and get behind him and boot
his butt all the way home. Should have been home an hour ago.
Should have been here so he could keep an eye on you while I
start fixing dinner. Look at him just sauntering down Cassina
Way like he owns it and got all the time in the world. Your sister be up in a minute and yelling soon as her eyes open and him
just taking his own sweet time.

He won too. Got a little change in his pocket. Tell by the
way he walks. Walking like he got a load in his pants, like
other people's nickels and dimes weigh him down. (. . .) Never
saw a man get sour-faced and down in the mouth when he
wins.

The Marriage of Bette and Boo

Christopher Durang

Play
20s
Comic
Contemporary

Enter Bette, still in her wedding dress.

Hurry up, Boo. I want to use the shower. *(To the audience.)* First I was a tomboy. I used to climb trees and beat up my brother Tom. Then I used to try to break my sister Joanie's voice box because she liked to sing. She always scratched me though, so instead I tried to play Emily's cello. Except I don't have a lot of musical talent, but I'm very popular. And I know more about the cello than people who don't know anything. I don't like the cello, it's too much work and besides, keeping my legs open that way made me feel funny. I asked Emily if it made her feel funny and she didn't know what I meant; and then when I told her she cried for two whole hours and then went to confession twice, just in case the priest didn't understand her the first time. Dopey Emily. She means well. *(Calls offstage.)* Booey! I'm pregnant! *(To audience.)* Actually I couldn't be, because I'm a virgin. A married man tried to have an affair with me, but he was married, and so it would have been point-less. I didn't know he was married until two months ago. Then I met Booey, sort of on the rebound. He seems fine though. (. . .) *(Giddy, happy.)* Booey, come on!

Mines

Susan Straight

Short Story
30s
Dramatic
Contemporary

Clarette works at the youth prison, where her nephew is incarcerated. The title comes from something her young nephew said: "I'ma get mines, all I gotta say, Aunti Clarette. (. . .) I ain't working all my life for some shitty car and a house. I'ma get mines now."

The Chicano fools have gang names on the sides of their skulls. The white fools have swastikas. The Vietnamese fools have writing I can't read. And the black fools—if they're too dark, they can't have anything on their heads. Maybe on the lighter skin at their chest, or the inside of the arm.

Where I sit for the morning shift at my window, I can see my nephew in his line, heading to the library. Square-head light-skinned fool like my brother. Little dragon on his skull. Nothing in his skull. Told me it was cause he could breathe fire if he had to. Alfonso tattooed on his right arm.

"What, he too gotdamn stupid to remember his own name?" my godfather said when he saw it. "Gotta look down by his elbow every few minutes to check?" (. . .)

One Chicano kid has PERDONEME MI ABUELITA in fancy cursive on the back of his neck. Sorry my little grandma. I bet that makes her feel much better.

When my nephew shuffles by, he grins and says softly, "Hey, Auntie Clarette."

I want to slap the dragon off the side of his stupid skull.

The Morgan Yard

Kevin O'Morrison

Play
40
Dramatic
Contemporary

Orpha Morgan Reinhart, owner of the largest undertaking business in the town of Indian Landing, Missouri, vents to her mother about the family graveyard.

This place, this place, this place—God damn this place! Ever since I can remember, it's been this place! When we weren't tending graves up here, or burying somebody, we were planning to come up here. We had picnics up here, weddings up here, even for Christsakes, christenings up here! Cradle to the grave, Morgan style! And you—up here every chance you could get, talking to Daddy like he was still alive—(*Fights tears.*)—everybody in town calling you the crazy woman. You see these pins—(*Points to pins on her bosom.*) This one is Daughters of 1812. This one's Daughters of the Confederacy. (*Blazing.*) If it wasn't for you, I'd be president of both—instead of the daughter of a damned old fool! (*Fights tears again.*) Letting Daddy cough his goddam lungs out up there on that old farm—you could have brought us down to town to live instead of waiting till he died! And don't give me that guff about him wanting to die up there—he was *sick*, you could have made him! (*Sees her father clearly before her.*) Day after day, laying out there under that goddam sycamore, coughing, coughing—his skin growing so waxy you could see his bones right through it. (*Final tug at her white gloves.*) I'm going now, Mama. And if I ever see this place again, I hope it's plowed under. (*She goes.*)

My Father's Girlfriend

Irene Ziegler

Novel
35-45
Dramatic
Contemporary

Della Shiftlet has been accused of murdering Annie's father. When Annie confronts Della in prison, they meet for the first time.

You must be Annie. I'm Della Shiftlet. *(Striking a pose.)* Ta-daa. *(Pause.)* Excuse my appearance. I look like death in orange. You don't happen to have a rattail comb you could slip me, do you, maybe inside a hollow Bible or something? They took mine.

Oh, well. I'd probably stab somebody with it, anyway. *(Pause.)* That was a joke.

Honey, I promise you. I did not kill your father. He could be a pain in the ass, but dammit, I loved the son of a bitch. Pete Duncan wants me to admit to a murder I didn't do, and I won't. Maybe pleading guilty to second-degree murder will save me from the chair, but it won't save me from jail, and it won't let me keep the property that your daddy, of sound mind and body, willed to me. My life goes down the toilet, Annie. I got nothin' but an orange jumpsuit and a tin cup. And why? Because I loved your father, and wanted to live out the rest of my life with him in a little house on a sleepy lake. For that, my life is ruined. Now you answer me this: Is that all right with you?

Just talk to Pete Duncan. That's all I'm asking.

My Girlish Days

Karen L. B. Evans

Play
20s
Dramatic
Contemporary

It's 1936 in Hallsboro, North Carolina. Gertie shares with her friend Jenny the uncertain feelings of new love for Sam.

It scared me, too. What I'm trying to say is I don't know what's going on between me and Sam. At first I could keep him at arm's length, and I was cold and I was mean. Thought he was trying to add another notch to his belt. But he kept coming back for more, like a dog with a bone, he wouldn't let go, and the worse I treated him the nicer he was. And then he kissed me. And I couldn't hear Mama telling me to walk with God, and I couldn't hear Miss Esther Norcum asking me to do my homework over the way she taught it. When he touches me, nothing matters. And I don't understand . . . and I'm scared.

My Left Breast
Susan Miller

Play
40s
Dramatic
Contemporary

*A cancer survivor—heartbroken at a failed relationship—
reflects on life thereafter.*

When you have a brush with death, you think, if I pull through
this, I'm going to do it all differently. I'm going to say exactly
what I think. I'll be a kind and generous citizen. I won't be
impatient with my son. I won't shut down to my lover. I'll
learn to play the trumpet. I'll never waste another minute.

Then you don't die. And it's God, I hate my hair! Would you
please pick up your clothes! How long do we have to stand in
this fucking line?

One day I'm sitting in a café and a man with ordinary difficulties is complaining. Our water heater is on the fritz. Just like
that he says it. OUR something isn't working and WE are wor-
rying about it.

I want to say—cherish the day your car broke down, the water
pump soured, the new bed didn't arrive on time. Celebrate the
time you got lost and maps failed. On your knees to this
domestic snafu, you blessed pair. While you can still feel the
other's skin in the night, her foot caressing your calf, preoccu-
pations catching on the damp sheets. You twist, haul an arm
over. Remote kisses motor your dreams.

Never Kick a Man When He's Down

Norman Bert and Deb Bert

Original Monologue
Late 30s
Dramatic
Contemporary

Beatrice, a middle-aged woman, speaks with a policeman at a police station interview room.

I don't know why I'm here. Really. Just— I had to get out of there. (*Pause.*) We been married forty-five years. He was a police officer, just like you, and he worked hard so that we could have. You can write *that* in your report. (*Pause.*) It started with his drinkin'. Well, it *is* Christmas, ya' know? (*Deep breath.*) This time it was Rick. Erwin went downstairs, and he saw Rick's clothes all over the floor, and he—huh?—Oh, Rick's my son. He lives downstairs. Huh? Oh, he's uh, lessee, uh forty. Yeah, forty. (*Pause.*) So Erwin yells at me. He starts out just goin' over it and goin' over it: "God damned kid's lazy like a damned Indian. Lives just like a damned Indian." Then he'd get down into my face and just spit, "It's all your fault, damn it!" Then he came up behind me and whispered in my ear. "Oooooh, I could just kill you." It was like, like— I didn't know him. "And you know I'll do it too," he says. "Pop!" he says with his finger pokin' me in the back of my head. "Pop! You'll hear the bullet comin' too, by God." (*Pause.*) So I—I left. My daughter made me, when she heard. She made me come here. (*Pause.*) I'm not gonna sign your papers there. He's not like that. I can't have him arrested. I can't do that. He's just down now. I'd never kick a man when he's down.

Night Luster

Laura Harrington

Play
20s
Dramatic
Contemporary

A young woman longs to be seen.

I don't think people see me. I get this feeling sometimes like I'm invisible or something. I can be standing there in a room and I'm talking and everything, and it's like my words aren't getting anywhere and I look down at myself and Jesus, sometimes my body isn't getting anywhere either. It's like I'm standing behind a one-way mirror and I can see the guys and I can hear the guys, but they can't see me and they can't hear me. And I start to wonder if maybe I'm ugly or something, like maybe I'm some alien species from another planet and I don't speak the language and I look totally weird. But I don't know this, you see, because on this other planet I had this really nice mother who told me I was beautiful and that I had a voice to die for because she loved me so much, not because it was true. And I arrive here on Earth and I'm so filled with her love and her belief in me that I walk around like I'm beautiful and I sing like I have a voice to die for. And because I'm so convinced and so strange and so deluded, people pretend to listen to me—because they're being polite or something—or maybe they're afraid of me. And at first I don't notice because I sing with my eyes closed. But then one day I open my eyes and find out I'm living in this world where nobody sees me and nobody hears me. (*Beat.*) I'm just looking' for that one guy who's gonna hear me, see me, really take a chance. I mean, I hear them. I'm listening so hard I hear promises when somebody's just sayin' hello. Jesus, if anybody ever heard what I've got locked up inside me . . . I'd be a star.

'Night, Mother
Marsha Norman

Play
Late 30s, early 40s
Dramatic
Contemporary

Suicidal Jessie matter-of-factly describes her current outlook to her mother.

You know I couldn't work. I can't do anything. I've never been around people my whole life, except when I went to the hospital. I could have a seizure any time. What good would a job do? The kind of job I could get would make me feel worse. (. . .)

It's true! (. . .)

And I can't do anything either, about my life, to change it, make it better, make me feel better about it. Like it better, make it work. But I can stop it. Shut it down, turn it off like the radio when there's nothing on I want to listen to. It's all I really have that belongs to me and I'm going to say what happens to it. And it's going to stop. And I'm going to stop it. So. Let's just have a good time.

no known country

Steven Schutzman

Play
35
Dramatic
Contemporary

*Emily—a lonely American physician working in a war-torn
foreign country—is in a cave, tipsy from booze. She speaks
to a woman whose cynicism about love inspires Emily to
defend her dreams.*

I want to get married. I want my rightful portion. I want to
marry that little Doctor and have a boy and a girl with him by
natural childbirth without the use of painkilling drugs and send
pictures of our beautiful family to friends and relatives every
New Year with a personal greeting we write ourselves. Our
children, Greg and Marcia, will be outgoing, charming and
interested in adults. Marcia will not reach puberty early. Greg
will not have Attention Deficit Disorder. I will recover quickly
from childbirth. My butt, my butt, the Doctor will love my butt
through all its changes over the years. Every few months the
Doctor and I will stay up all night talking over a bottle of wine.
Neither of us will take lovers, it won't even cross our minds. I
want to show my father that his abuse of me made me stronger
than any man. Oh . . . I want my true inheritance. I want to
gloat. I want to kill my father. I don't want to be in this foreign
country trying to cure the ills of the world. I'm ill. I'm mentally
ill. I need constant soothing, deep healing and multiple orgasms
from a Doctor. I want my rightful portion. I want to kill my
father but he's already dead and the dead fuck didn't even have
the decency to stick around to attend my college graduation,
Harvard, Phi Beta Kappa, 1990. I want to kill all men. I want
to own my body again. Hey, Mr. Doctor, I want to get married.

The Norbals
Brian Drader

Play
60s
Seriocomic
Contemporary

Frieda Norbal has gathered the clan together for Christmas; her son Danny and his wife Penny are broke, her son Randall is narcoleptic, Bee is in the middle of a sex change and has brought her lesbian lover, Connie, along for support. And Sean, the youngest, overdosed on morphine on the eve of their celebration. In the midst of these multiple crises, Frieda takes a moment to talk to Samantha, Randall's latest girlfriend.

I've known about Connie and Bee for at least a year now, but I must say it took me a while to make the connection. I knew Connie was a lesbian, but at the time we thought Bee was gay, and she just liked to dress up now and again . . . that's what Bee thought too, until she met Connie . . . so naturally we just assumed they were best friends. Bee didn't tell us different. But the last time they came to see us in Winnipeg, Bee had these breasts, and when I hugged her, they moved. I felt them squish up against my chest. Her fake breasts had never moved like that before. A mother notices these things.

Odd, isn't it? You get such a preconceived notion of who your children are . . . based on what, I don't know . . . little scraps of detail that you impose significance on . . . and when they start to veer off, when they become somebody else, you can't even see it. You set them, like a hairdo, and they're not allowed to change.

I never knew Sean did drugs. I didn't know he had anything to do with them. It was a complete surprise to me.

I love my family. I love them more than myself, but sometimes I look around and all I see are strangers. The children I raised, the man I married, they're strangers. I don't know who they are. And without them, I'm nobody. A batty old woman chasing after stories to fill her life up with.

Normalcy

Don Nigro

Play
19
Comic
Contemporary

Madison, a college student, presents a report on her favorite president.

OK, so my report is on my favorite president
which was Warren G. Harding who was a
very great president from Ohio which is
called the Mother of Presidents or some
kind of Mother or wait maybe that's
Virginia, I'll have to look that up.
But anyway Warren G. Harding was
from Marion, Ohio, where he edited
a newspaper and had a very nice haircut
and there was a rumor he was secretly
half octoroon or something obscurely
ethnic which I think would be really
cool if it was true but was probably
frowned on at the time by respectable people
who let's face it are generally a bunch of
ignorant sheep-faced bigots even the best
of them a little bit although I have a hard time
believing it was true because then
why would he get down on his knees
in the White House late one night and
swear allegiance to the Ku Klux Klan

which apparently he did although
in all fairness to the president
he was probably drunk at the time
because President Harding although
a very great man and a wonderful president
used to drink like the world was coming to
an end next Tuesday and once showed up
at this important dinner with disgruntled
labor leaders rip-roaring dead skunk
drunk, sat down on the cake
and announced that Susan B. Anthony
had a really nice ass.

Not About Nightingales

Tennessee Williams

Play
Early 20s
Dramatic
Contemporary

Riots have just broken out in the prison in which Eva works.
The inmate she loves is about to jump out of a window to
escape punishment for his part in the riot.

Oh, Jim, I would have liked to live with you outside. We might
have found a place where searchlights couldn't point their find-
ers at us when we kissed. I would have given you so much
you've never had. Quick love is hard. It gives so little pleasure.
We should have had long nights together with no walls. Or no
stone walls—I know the place! A tourist camp beside a highway, Jim, with all night long the great trucks rumbling by—but
only making shadows through the blinds! I'd touch the stone
you're made of, Jim, and make you warm, so warm, so terribly
warm your love would burn a scar upon my body that no
length of time could heal!—Oh, Jim, if we could meet like that,
at some appointed time, some place decided now, where we
could love in secret and be warm, protected, not afraid of
things—We could forget all this as something dreamed!—Where
shall it be? When, Jim? Tell me before you go! Tell me where.

Notes from the Edge Conference

Roy Blount, Jr.

Essay
30s
Comic
Contemporary

At the Edge Conference, everything is edgy.

My friend and I were talking. I'm saying like who is your best rock star and who is your best this star and that star and it hits us, all our best ones like live out near the edge. And we're talking you know and I go, "That's why you like me. I'm out near the edge."

And he goes like he's not believing me, he goes, "Yeah?"

I go, "Yeah."

"So what's it look like over there?" he goes.

I go, "You put your toes out over it and look out and down and you feel something pressing up evenly on each one of your toes, toe toe toe toe toe, and you see somebody looking out and up at you." Because—

And I don't know what hit him, he goes like "*Yeah*! Oh, *yeah*! Oh *yeah*, Lori! Sure, Lori!" and goes out and rents this motel room somewhere and tears it up.

Number

David J. LeMaster

Original Monologue
20s
Seriocomic
Contemporary

Oh, the magic of math . . .

I have this really great trick I want to show you. Think of a number between one and ten. Come on, it's fun. OK? Now. Take the number five. Is that your number? I didn't think so. But take your number and either add or subtract five. If it's higher or lower than five. Add . . . You know. Right. So have you done it? Good. Now. Think of that number. And multiply it by two. You don't need scratch paper, do you? OK. Anyway. Multiply by two. Now divide by four. Are you following me? Look, this is not a math test. You are so stupid sometimes. Have you got the fricking number yet? All right. Now add ten and subtract the number of times you've slept with Frank.

Uh, huh. That's what I thought. You didn't even flinch when I said it. Because you have, haven't you? Even though you're my best friend. All this time I thought I was fighting some unknown babe, and I was really fighting you. Benedictus Arnoldess.

So look. Take that number you came up with, right? I want you to take that number you came up with. And I want you to remember it. And every time you hear it, I want you to think about me.

Spoils a good number, doesn't it?

Olivia

Dorothy Strachey

Short Story
30s+
Dramatic
Contemporary

Olivia remembers a powerful adolescent crush.

Now I was all moroseness and gloom—heavy-hearted, leaden-footed. I could take no interest in my lessons; it was impossible to think of them. (. . .) I sat for hours, my arms folded on the table in front of me, my head resting on them, plunged in a kind of coma.

"What on earth are you doing, Olivia?" a friend would ask. "Are you asleep?"

"Oh, leave me alone," I would cry impatiently. "I'm thinking."

But I wasn't thinking. I was sometimes dreaming—the foolish dreams of adolescence: of how I should save her life at the cost of my own by some heroic deed, of how she would kiss me on my deathbed, of how I should kneel at hers and what her dying word would be, of how I should become famous by writing poems which no one would know were inspired by her, of how one day she would guess it, and so on and so on. (. . .)

If only I could express myself—in words, in music, anyhow. I imagined myself a prima donna or a great actress. Oh, heavenly relief! Oh, an outlet for all this ferment which was boiling within me! Perilous stuff! If I could only get rid of it—shout it to the world—declaim it away!

One-Dimensional Person

Jason Milligan

Original Monologue
Teens-20s
Comic
Contemporary

A young woman stares in shock at her best friend.

Wow. I . . . that's all I can say, "Wow." *(Beat.)* I mean, I knew you were going for a "new look," Stacey, but . . . well, I mean . . . *(Trying to be nice.)* I dunno if that's quite it. I mean, it's very . . . unique . . . and you certainly do look like a "new person" . . . but you kind of look like a new dead person or something. I just never thought of you as the "Goth" type. *(Beat.)* Oh, that's not Goth? What is it supposed to be, then? *(Beat.)* "Nouveau Wiccan?" Right . . . *(Shakes her head.)* Listen, I know you're looking around for a "cause" . . . something to make your life meaningful . . . but this comes across more like a *fad* than a life's purpose. I mean, what is your heart telling you to do, Stacey? *(Beat, then rolls her eyes.)* No, it's not telling you to "ditch the planet," where did you even get that from, anyway? Stacey, we used to work side by side in the soup kitchen, remember? Volunteering on Thanksgiving Day? You had such a sense of purpose in your life, such a desire to help other people . . . and now . . . I dunno, you just seem so . . . well, I'm just going to come right out and say it . . . self-involved. *(Beat.)* Well, I'm sorry, but I'm supposed to be your best friend, I'd rather tell you the truth than stand here and B.S. you. You're turning into a one-dimensional person, Stacey! Someone who's a cardboard cutout, who other people make fun of! *(Beat.)* Fine. If that's the way you feel about it. But if you wake up one day and look in the mirror . . . and decide to wash out the purple rinse and take all those earrings out . . . I'll still be here. Because. That's what friends are really about.

The One-Eyed Guru
Andrew Biss

Play
30s
Dramatic
Contemporary

Rachel, having returned home unusually late, confronts her husband, Jack, who has been anxiously waiting.

(Proffering a scarf.) Here, take it. It's Melanie's. *(Beat.)* Yes, Jack, Melanie's—I know it's hers. I know it from that pungent smell of a Chanel No. 5 knockoff. That and the fact that I found the tail end of it poking out from beneath our bed. *(Beat.)* I've seen her wearing it often. It's obviously a favorite. Which is why I'm sure she'd be very relieved to have it returned. *(Beat.)* And no, this didn't make me feel any better, Jack . . . having you wait up into the night, wondering all the time where I was? Having nasty, insidious thoughts clawing their way into your mind as you tried like a fool to pretend to yourself that everything was all right? No, it didn't. Not really. *(Beat.)* But perhaps . . . perhaps if everybody knew but *you*; perhaps if *you* had *your* friends telling you that you were being made a mockery of; perhaps if *you'd* had the phone slammed down on you a dozen times the moment your voice was heard on the other end; perhaps if you'd smelled cheap perfume on your husband's jacket, on his shirts, on the sheets, in the car, up your nose, always, everywhere, lined to the inside of your nostrils like some noxious chemical you couldn't escape no matter where you went, no matter what you did, then yes, *yes* . . . I might have felt better.

The Oxcart

René Marqués

Play
40+
Dramatic
Contemporary

Doña Gabriela dreams of returning to her native Puerto Rico.

Because now I know what was happening to us all. The curse of the land! The land is sacred. The land cannot be abandoned. We must go back to what we left behind so that the curse of the land won't pursue us any more. And I'll return with my son to the land from where we came. And I'll sink my hands in the red earth of my village just as my father sunk his to plant the seeds. And my hands will be strong again. And my house will smell once more of patchouli and peppermint. And there'll be land outside. Four acres to share. Even though that's all! It's good land. It's land. It's land that gives life. Only four acres. Even if they're not ours!

Patient A

Lee Blessing

Play
Early 20s
Dramatic
Contemporary

Kimberly Bergalis, infected with HIV by her dentist, remembers the final moments before her death.

[M]y mom brought up a good point. She said, "Why are you so sure that it's not going to get any worse? That it's going to be a quiet death, and not some more terrible thing? (. . .)" And that's something I never thought about. I just thought how *I* can't take this pain anymore, and how *I* feel about this pain, and how *I* want to be out of my misery before it gets worse. But God might not take me now. So that made me think. Well, anyway, the priest was really nice, and he gave me the Sacrament of the Sick, which I discovered I'd been getting all along at church, at weekly Mass. It's the exact same thing. And he gave me First Holy Communion, and then he left and I just felt so good suddenly. I started thinking again about the cemetery where I was going to be buried, and all the names— (. . .)

And how I'm going to lie right next to my grandmother on top of that mountain— (. . .)

And how I'm going to lift up and just fly away into the heavens— (. . .)

And how God's going to come down and take my hand— (. . .)

And how my body's just going to be this thing I used while I was on this Earth. (. . .)

Anyway, then this peace came over me, and I was able to sleep.

The Patron Saint of Jello

Nell Grantham

Original Monologue
30+
Comic
Contemporary

Somewhere in North Dakota, Elsie is at a Lutheran Church picnic, amidst much Tupperware.

[And Pastor Larson] was there. Along with little Lars and his wife Sonja. They had stopped by after handbell choir to check on Hulda what with her sprained wrist and all, and what did they find but Irv drinking Jagermeister and swearing at the hockey game, and his boy Thor playing at the Dungeons and Dragons. Right there in the rumpus room! (. . .)

Let's see what do we got here? (. . .)

Oh, I didn't have a lot of time so it's just Glorified Rice. I was going to make those little smokies with the grape jelly and barbeque sauce in the Crock-Pot, but then the boys went and ate 'em all up when I wasn't looking. Little buggers. (. . .)

Yeah, it might turn out to be the next big recipe, ya never know. Remember the first time Doris brought that Frog Eye salad? It was all green and had that macaroni that nobody could say. (. . .)

But then we all gave it a try and by golly, it was a keeper! So don't you worry about your lime circus peanut salad—(. . .) I'm sure it will be gobbled up in no time.

The Patron Saint of Jello

Nell Grantham

Original Monologue
30+
Comic
Contemporary

Somewhere in North Dakota, Elsie is at a Lutheran Church picnic, amidst much Tupperware.

Say what you like about them Easterners but that one, she can drive a tractor straight as a yardstick from here to Tuesday. (. . .)

And, you know what she named that baby? (. . .)

Well, everybody just thought they'd name him Aud, like all the Opperude men and his dad before him. But Oppy (who never used his given name), he said "No way, no doin." He'd taken enough guff about his name and jokes about his dad bein' odd "O-D-D" that he wasn't going to saddle the little guy with the same name. He said he wanted the boy to have a normal name. An American name. (. . .)

Yeah! (. . .)

This gal Amy she says to Oppy, she says, "If you're gonna move me out here to Karlsruhe on the prairie, and you expect me to make that stinky lutefisk for Christmas dinner, AND you propose to me at a Sons of Norway fish fry, by Golly our boy is getting a Norske name. (. . .)

Yeah. They named him Trigve. (. . .)

Trigve Sundeen Opperude. Trigve from some Norsk legend she read about and Sundeen after her folks. (. . .)

Yeah!

Patter for the Floating Lady

Steve Martin

Play
25-35
Dramatic
Contemporary

Magically suspended in the air, Angie recounts her failed relationship with a magician.

Oh yes, I loved you. So many things. Safety, words exchanged, letters. I would cough and the phone would ring and it would be you, asking if I was all right. You could imitate me and make me laugh. You would buy me a little thing. When I made spaghetti for you, you were so grateful, Pavarotti himself couldn't have made better spaghetti. We were at a restaurant and a woman came up to you, flirting and right there in front of her, you laced your fingers between mine, showing her who you loved.

But the most powerful was the tennis shoe. My God, I cried. After our week in the tropics—where we collapsed, ended—a month later, not having spoken, you sent me a tennis shoe. I looked at it for days, not knowing why you sent it. Then one morning, barefoot, not knowing why, I slipped my foot into it. Sand. Grains of sand still in it from seven thousand miles away; each one the size of a memory. I will love you forever for that second. I cried. I cried for us. But when we fell apart, you didn't understand that I would be back. That if you let me have my life, I would be with you forever. But everything you said and did, every touch at night in bed, every kindness, every loving comment had this sentence attached: Maybe now she'll love me. And it made you weak. And if I'm not going to love someone strong, why love at all?

Perfect Body
Cynthia Meier

Play
30+
Dramatic
Contemporary

An actress rails against the body consciousness of her profession.

I am so angry. Angry that this bullshit I've listened to my whole life was ever even said to me:

Cindy, I care about you. If only you'd lose weight . . . BULLSHIT.

Cindy, you have such a pretty face, if only . . . BULLSHIT.

Cindy, you have so much talent, if only . . . BULLSHIT.

Cindy, if only for your health . . . BULLSHIT.

Being pulled aside by well-meaning friends, approached by strangers in the grocery store, counseled by teachers, lectured by relatives, talked to by theater directors, "How much weight could you lose by opening night?"

BULLSHIT.

I am an actress. Whatever else I may be in the world, I am an actress. I might have been a great classical actress. I lost a hundred pounds to play Blanche DuBois. The reviewer in the city paper said I was too hefty for the part. What do you do when you have the soul of Juliet in what others perceive as the body of her nurse? There are a few successful fat actresses. But they are, by and large, comic figures. I am not. Perhaps in classical Greece I would have made it. Here and now, I don't even try.

Personal History
Dominic Taylor

Play
30+
Dramatic
Contemporary

Bethany's grief over a destroyed stained glass window comes from an intimately personal place.

Gene? Gene where did you go? What you looking for? Where are we going? Gene get back in here.

(Picks up a piece of glass.)

Did I ever tell you what Momma said about stained glass? Are you listening? I was a baby, maybe four and I asked Momma, why did they have colored windows at church? She said that they were special. See, Momma said that, God listens to all prayers, but when you pray in front of a stained glass window, it's like you are placing an emergency call. It's like, this is the most important time. She used to say not to pray in front of them unless you need something very badly. But when you need something badly, that's where you go.

Gene, you listening?

But then when it's broken, do you pray to where it once was? What do you do then? Pray to the glass. Gene? What do you do then?

The Piano Lesson

August Wilson

Play
30s
Dramatic
Contemporary

Berniece lashes out at her suitor, a preacher.

You trying to tell me a woman can't be nothing without a man. But you alright, huh? You can just walk out of here without me—without a woman—and still be a man. That's alright. Ain't nobody gonna ask you, "Avery, who you got to love you?" That's alright for you. But everybody gonna be worried about Berniece. "How Berniece gonna take care of herself? How she gonna raise that child without a man? Wonder what she do with herself. How she gonna live like that?" Everybody got all kinds of questions for Berniece. Everybody telling me I can't be a woman unless I got a man. Well, you tell me, Avery—you know—how much woman am I?

Population Growth

Aoise Stratford

Play
Late 20s
Comic
Contemporary

Charlotte, talked into a blind date, waits nervously for the guy to show up.

My best friend. (. . .) Donna is big on moral support. Donna's idea of moral support is to escort you, with a vice-like grip to whichever place she thinks you should be and then to block the door with her body so you can't get away. (. . .) This whole miserable experience has been Donna's idea. In fact, most of the true clunkers, the real this-was-a-bad-idea-why-don't-I-shoot myself-now-and save-us-all-a-lot-of-trouble moments in my life . . . most of them, can be traced back to Donna. For example, when we were twelve, Donna had me sign up for our high-school "Dare Devil Talent and Magic Night," because she thought it would help me get a boyfriend. My act, carefully planned by Donna, was to juggle scissors. Why? Because boys love girls who flirt with danger. I don't need to tell you how that went. Oh, and here's another favorite: hiding a ziplock bag of vodka infused watermelon chunks down the front of my prom dress. That was also Donna's idea. (. . .) You'd think, given the size of the world's population, I'd have less trouble choosing people to hang out with, but somehow I've been stuck to Donna like white on rice since grade school. She's my best friend. Did I mention that? Sometimes I hate her.

The Primary English Class

Israel Horovitz

Play
20s
Comic
Contemporary

Debbie Wastba, on her first day of teaching, must address a roomful of children who speak different languages, none of them English.

Listen now, I'll just go really slow. (*Pauses, smiles.*) My name is Debbie Wastba. (*Writes her name on blackboard.*) W-A-S-T-B-A. That's pronounced Wass-tah-bah: Wastba. (*Links each of the three syllables together on board, in the following way: WA ST BA*) Think of Wah as in wah-tah. Splash. Splash. Stah as in stah-bility. And Bah as in Bah-dum . . . as in (*Sings "Dragnet" theme.*) Bum-tah-bum-bum. Well, listen. It was literally double its length in its ancient, biblical form. (*Pause.*) Actually, that tune was wrong. It would be much more like . . . (*Sings again, to tune of "My Funny Valentine."*) Bum bum-bum- bum-bum-bum . . . bum bum-bum bum-bum-bum . . . bum bum-bum-baaahhhmmmmmmm . . . (*Pauses: sees they are confused.*) Well, anyway, really, you can easily check your Bibles if you want.

The Primary English Class

Israel Horovitz

Play
20s
Comic
Contemporary

Debbie Watsba, on her first day, must teach primary English to a roomful of children, all of whom speak different languages, none of them English.

(*Rummages through stack of papers on desk, holds up lesson plan.*) This is our lesson plan. That's lesson . . . plan. Lesson plan. We're going to be together for several hours and I thought it would be highly professional and competent for me to make a plan. And I did. And here it is: (*Reads, smiling confidently.*) One. A pleasant welcome and normal chatter. For two, I've planned your basic salutation, such as the goods—good morning, good afternoon, good night, good luck, and good grief. (*Laughs.*) That was a mildly amusing joke: "good grief." Later in the night—after we've learned a bit of English—you'll be able to, well, get the joke. (*Pauses.*) Let's move along. Three will be basic customs: ours here. (*Reading again.*) Four will be a short history of our English language. (*As the students take their notes, they, as we, begin to realize that Wastba is only writing the numbers one through six on the blackboard—no words. They raise their hands in question, but she waves them away, barging ahead.*) Five will be the primary lesson on the primary English class, according to the book. And six will be the very essential verb "to be." At some point, we shall also inspect the very basic concept of silence. (*Smiles.*) Now then, as you can see, there are only six points to cover and hours and hours ahead in which to cover them. (*All stare blankly at her smiling face.*) Now then: Questions?

A Private Practise

Andrew Biss

Play
50s
Comic
Contemporary

Mrs. Flagg, a housewife, pays a visit to a psychiatrist who is trying to ascertain her level of sexual maturity.

Oral copulation? No . . . no, it doesn't repulse me. But then, I can't say that the thought of it appeals to me, either—all that equipment in my mouth. And I have heard it can be very painful. I'm told it's the actual attachment of the tooth to the root cavity that's the worst part. Still, I'm sure it's worth it not to have the bother of dentures. And they're so well trained these days, aren't they? *(Beat.)* Mind you, you've got to be careful. Some of them get up to all sorts once they've got you in the chair. Criminal, some of the things I've heard. Absolutely unrepeatable. Take Beryl at the end of our street—went in to have her wisdoms removed and ended up several months later with more than her face ballooning up, if you know what I mean. She had a whiff of suspicion the next day, when the numbness wore off. Said she felt sore in an area where dentists aren't generally known for putting their tools. She kept [the baby], though. Raymond, I think she called it. Funny-looking thing. His ears were different sizes. Mind you, she was always a bit peculiar—I wouldn't have been surprised if it had had two heads.

A Private Practise

Andrew Biss

Play
50s
Comic
Contemporary

Mrs. Flagg, a housewife, relates the tragic death of her previous husband to a psychiatrist.

Well, I suppose there's no harm in telling you. You see, my first husband—Lance—was a guinea pig for penile implants. He was on the cutting edge of technology. Much like yourself. But they were early days and not all the wrinkles had been ironed out. Anyway, one evening, while he was watching the swimsuit segment of the Miss World contest, I heard a bloodcurdling scream coming from the living room—turned out his device had malfunctioned and impaled him to the back of the sofa! (*With a quavering voice.*) By the time the ambulance arrived it was all over. (*Dabbing her eyes with a tissue.*) Awful, it was . . . just awful. (*Puts the tissue back into her handbag.*) The manufacturers were very understanding, of course. They awarded me a lump sum of considerable size and a new, brand-name three-piece suit. No rubbish, mind you—top quality plush. Lovely to the touch, too. (*A sigh.*) Yes, I'm afraid Lance paid a very stiff price for his pioneer spirit.

Rat Bohemia
Sarah Schulman

Novel
20s-30s
Comic
Contemporary

Killer, speaking to her best friend, Rita, rails against the loss of civility.

You know, Rita. You know how it is. Some people, you call them and they never call you back. Even if they've known you for a long time. I'd like to call those people up and say, *Listen, Mack, if you ever call me I will call you right away. If I call you I want you to call me back. Don't snub me or I'll kill you. Don't snub me.* Of course you can't go around saying *I'll kill you* to people or they'll never call you back. Plus, they'll tell other people you said that and then the others won't call either. The murderous intention has to be simply but subtly understood.

Rats

Migdalia Cruz

Play
Late 20s-early 30s
Dramatic
Contemporary

This is from a collection of monologues recording the experiences of Puerto Rican women growing up in the South Bronx.

I'm the only Puerto Rican in New Canaan, Connecticut. I figure as long as I don't open my mouth I'm safe. I was at a party once and some WASPy lady in tennis whites asked if I was from England. England?! Can you imagine?! She said she thought I was from England because I had an accent. She looked real surprised when I told her I was from the South Bronx. "South what?" But once she got used to the idea, it seemed quite wonderful and she grabbed my elbow and brought me around to all of her friends. "Have you met this wonderful creature yet? She's from the Bronx—the South Bronx!" "Amazing! Is anybody still living there?" No—nobody important . . . just people. My mother my father, my sisters. The priest who gave me first communion. My friend Sharon whose little brother Junie died of sickle cell anemia when we were twelve and he was ten. (. . .)

The Bronx—where people talk with such intriguing accents.

Renea

Theresa Carilli

Original Monologue
30s
Dramatic
Contemporary

Renea, a serious, stern, humorless woman, has just stolen her lover's car and now accounts for her erratic behavior.

From the moment I met her, I knew she'd leave me. Usually I don't mind because my life has been a series of comings and goings. My father was a military man and he thought it prudent for me and my siblings never to develop strong feelings. Feelings are fleeting. They come and they go. They turn you upside down and they disappear. They leave you in agony. They make you think you are a monster. But feelings are not real. They are only moments of being far too extremely human. And then if you have the unfortunate opportunity to reflect upon your feelings, you realize that your feelings are an illusion—something you trick yourself into because they give you a hormonal high. I have never trusted feelings. Mine or anyone else's. And this is why it ended with Banda. Because of my unwillingness to trust the feelings I had for her and she had for me. (. . .) Perhaps you will find this particularly ironic when I tell you that I'm a therapist. See, most people think that therapists are in the business of tending to people's feelings but that's not true. We are in the business of teaching people how to manage their illusions.

The Right to Bare Arms (and Asses)

Elizabeth Wong

Play
30s+
Comic
Contemporary

Anina is a voluptuous blues singer in the tradition of the fabulous Etta James. She finishes her show-stopping number "Stand" on the other side of the curtain. Wild applause, she bows in her diva style, exits through the curtain into a backstage area.

What a show! What a show! Those people can't believe their eyes. A girl my size with my glorious thighs. Listen to them, they feel my love. Damn, I was cookin'! Oh yeah, uh huh. But who was that bitch was in the audience, with that clackety clackety knit one pearl two knitting in the front row shit. Where she think she is? Making some dog sweater during my show. Unbelievable! I'm glad I'm not one of those skinny needle knitting women. Men need something to hold onto, not a chicken bone with silicone. I don't have a lot of women as friends. Jealousy maybe, don't really know why. As a kid, I never got invited for sleepovers, pajama parties. And when my breasts happened, well, all my friends ended up being boys, men, and, oh, gay guys. Oh honey, you wish you could be me. I'm all that, and then some. Look at me. Uh huh. That's a fact. I have a spectacular body. That's right! I am soooo fine. Thick legs. Luscious hips. Look at these beauties. Still perky, and all one hundred percent ME!

Rights Wronged

Roger Nieboer

Play
Teen
Seriocomic
Contemporary

Megan explains to her friends why she was late for class, and the unfortunate result.

All I ate for breakfast was some Doritos and a Diet Cherry Coke and I wasn't feeling so great anyways. And I was already late for first period cuz I missed the bus, so I ran. Had to run all the way and by the time I got there it's already second period so I go to the office. Big Judy sends me to Bio Lab. Go directly to Bio Lab. Do not pass GO, do not collect two hundred dollars. Lab door's open. I sneak in. The teacher has a big plastic pail up there on the front table. He pops it open and this smell . . . this uggy-wamp, funeral parlor, odor of death permeates the entire supply of atmospheric oxygen. I'm thinking to myself, this is it: Gag City. The Big Barferoo. The teacher reaches into the bucket and goes, "Class, today we do frogs." And I go, "Whadya mean 'do'?" And he goes, "Dissection. We are going to begin the dissection of our frogs." And I go, "Whadya mean 'dissect'?" And he goes, "The systematic removal of tissues, organs, and . . . " And I go, "I can't." And he goes, "Why not?" And I'm all . . . "Well . . . . I'm a vegetarian." And he goes, "Young lady, I'm not asking you to eat the frog, but merely to observe its anatomical structure." And I go, "Can't I observe its anatomical structure without chopping it up into amphibian sushi?" At which point he launches into this big power-trip tirade, telling me that I'll never understand the glories and wonders of the human body if I don't slice and dice this poor, pickled creature. At which point I blow lunch all over the lab.

Romance
Barbara Lhota

Play
30s
Seriocomic
Contemporary

Miriam, a medieval literature professor, reveals to a stranger how she imagines her husband will react to her being missing, and in doing so, justifies leaving him.

I didn't mean he wouldn't be concerned. He's not that cold. He'd probably assume that he'd forgotten that I had one of my Literature Conferences. After a day, he'd figure out that the lovely sweet smell in our room comes from my powder spray, and he'd discover that he has to put his own tea on in the morning. By the second evening, he'd begin to miss the sound of Beethoven's *Moonlight Sonata* playing over and over with the taps of my typewriter. He laughs at the primitiveness of me still using one. And then he'd get a case of heartburn, but he wouldn't know why. He'd feel as if he'd lost something, but wouldn't know what. And then he'd remember that he'd felt as if I should be home by now. After which, he might feel a slight pang. A pang of longing. Longing for only me. But he'd brush it off quickly. So quickly. Too quickly. Finally, he'd call my mother. *(Pause, laughs sadly.)* And she'd get the helicopters out.

Roosters

Milcha Sanchez-Scott

Play
40
Seriocomic
Contemporary

As she works balls of tortilla dough, Chata, a hard boozer,
evaluates her history with men.

Ah, you people don't know what it is to eat fresh handmade
tortillas. My grandmother Hortensia, (. . .) would start making them at five o'clock in the morning. So the men would
have something to eat when they went into the fields. (. . .)
Every day at five o'clock she would wake me up. "Buenos
pinchi dias," she would say. I was twelve or thirteen years old,
still in braids. . . . "Press your hands into the dough," "Con
fuerza," "Put your stamp on it." One day I woke up, tú sabes,
con la sangre. "Ah! So you're a woman now. Got your own
cycle like the moon. Soon you'll want a man, well this is what
you do. When you see the one you want, you roll the tortilla
on the inside of your thigh and then you give it to him nice
and warm. Be sure you give it to him and nobody else." Well,
I been rolling tortillas on my thighs, on my nalgas, and God
only knows where else, but I've been giving my tortillas to the
wrong men . . . and that's been the problem with my life. First
there was Emilio. I gave him my first tortilla. Ay Mamacita, he
use to say, these are delicious. Aye, he was handsome, a real
lady-killer! After he did me the favor he didn't even have the
cojones to stick around . . . took my TV set too. They're
all shit.

A Russian Play

Don Nigro

Play
40
Dramatic
Contemporary

1900. Irina, a widow, lives on a crumbling Russian estate with her three daughters. She loves them, but she is jealous of their youth and beauty. She tries to persuade the local doctor, Radetsky, to marry her instead of one of them.

Now listen to me, you silly, silly man. What do you need? You need somebody to love you. To sleep with you. To cuddle up with you at night. To let you put your little mousie in her music box now and then. Well, I am just the person for that. If you marry me, you can noodle me all you want. All night and day if you like. I don't mind. Just as long as I can get up once in a while to make sure Igor feeds the chickens. You'll never have to make a fool of yourself again chasing young girls around who don't love you, grieving over them, wailing over them, getting shot in the ass over them. You can just be a happily married man for once. And you can live here with us instead of in that terrible filthy rat hole behind your office at the mental hospital. You're here most of the time anyway. Look here. Natasha doesn't love you. Katya hates you. And Anya is gone. A beautiful woman is giving herself to you here by the gazebo, and you have the gall to refuse me? Nobody refuses me. It's never happened and it never will. I am irresistible. And in your heart you know you've had just about all the rejection and humiliation you can stomach. So why don't you give up love forever and get married like a normal person?

Sans-Culottes in the Promised Land

Kirsten Greenidge

Play
20s
Seriocomic
Contemporary

Charlotte teaches a child whose parents are wealthy professionals. Here, she is talking to Lena, the family's nanny, who is illiterate.

Girrrrl. This family is *wacked.* I mean they are *gone*, oh my goodness. First I ring the bell for near to an hour before Broomhilda (*Mimics Carmel.*) answers the door and I'm like can I please talk to Lena, thank you very much—that cousin I have? She's gonna hook you up go-*od.* Literacy is legacy and all that so don't you worry but first I have to finish my story, 'cause then when I get into the kitchen the mother's like "Lena's *working,* you know"—*you know*—like we're on some English moor, like she's Some Parisian aristo-crat or some such non-sense—I minored in French Studies, I know a thing or two about those French rich people. Got their ass *whooped.* She wants to play some role? OK by me as long as I get a role, too. I'll be a sans-culotte, one of those French workers wanted to overthrow every-thang. You know what I'm saying? Natural rights, natural state; none of this abuse of wealth, of privilege, right? *Right?*

scatsong

Ernest Slyman

Play
20+
Dramatic
Contemporary

We're talkin' jaaaaaaazz.

In a Jazz Club, on MacDougal Street,
The horns blow cool, crazy, wild, talking up God,
Jumping in your brain, naughty and nice.
Trumpets feeling lucky, clapping a great bell —
Our ears flung wide like pearly gates,
Cause jazz teach us how to live,
And you hear a child call,
Saxophone chirp, hiccup, fart
And crying, rocking back,
Wicked, big mouth Mama kissing her baby, laughing, running
up and down your spine,
Bebop biting off your ear again and again, sweet tomorrow,
Naked, large truths bursting in your brain, zombie-eyed, God's
secret out, everybody know
Jazz eats you up, spits out your bones, cause what you say
don't mean nothing,
And here come that bliss, sorrow, guilt, sin kicking, chirping as
one big sound
Plucks you right up out of your skull, throws you down a hole,
And the deafness roars, sings like an atomic bomb,
And you so gone happy, frenzy loving, mad fool,
You slap your dead daddy and start running around with Jesus,
Until everything good and sacred,

Sticks you in the belly with a knife, takes out your appendix
And waves it in the air, jiggly fish,
(. . .) And upstairs, the musicians lay down their riffs,
Swing like birds chirping up the dawn,
Till everything we hold dear jabbers
Gloriously singing scat, scat, whodat,
And an great big orange sunrise
Swoops down and yaps in our bones,
Hurl us toward the soft fleshy dark.

Schoolgirl Figure
Wendy MacLeod

Play
17
Dramatic
Contemporary

Renee, an anorexic, decides to stay the course even though death from malnourishment lurks in the background, where a gurney is being set up.

Back in the days when I had muscles, I would rent a patch of ice every morning before it was light and go out there and try to master my school figures. I would fiercely skate that figure eight, because down the pike the school figures would count for 50 percent of my Olympic score. I practiced them even when I was on land, waiting in line for the water fountain, pressing my sneakers into imaginary blades. I spent the wee hours of my pre-pubescence obsessed with the Russian judge's good opinion of my outside edge and do you know what happened? They did away with the school figure part of the competition. Just did away with it. Because nobody saw them. Nobody wanted to see them. The audience just cared about the part where a skinny girl wears a skimpy leotard trimmed with maribou and jumps around to a disco version of *Carmen*. What can we learn from this? I'm sorry . . . ! forgot what I was going to say. Is it cold in here or is it just me? Oh, I know. What we have learned is that there is only so much in this world that we can control so by all means let us control what we can, achieve what we must. Perfection.

(When she speaks in rhyme we realize she's imagining herself in The Pantheon of dead girls.)

If you're happy with who you are
It's clearly time to raise the bar
Now it's time for my good-byeses
To you poor girls of the larger sizes

(A triumphant RENEE looks at the audience pityingly as she gets on the gurney. The gurney taxis her out.)

Self Defense, or death of some salesmen

Carson Kreitzer

Play
30s-40s
Dramatic
Contemporary

Jolene Palmer, a prostitute, is on death row for killing seven johns.

You feel something and you think that makes it real . . . I mean, I . . . I loved that woman like in all the fairy tales, you know? I usedta lay awake an' just listen to her breathe. An' she'd . . . turn over in her sleep, maybe, an' the feeling would just well up inside me.

Even if she's looking stupid and drooling on the pillow, still I'd just be all fulla this feeling of being in love. That this is it, you know, she's the one. What was she thinking, lying there in our bed, next to me in the dark? She's just thinkin', well, this'll do for now. Got a roof over my head. An' this crazy bitch willin' to go out and suck cock six, seven hours a day to take care a me.

What kind of a person . . . is that? That I was in love with. That I'm goin' to the chair because a her.

Self Defense, or death of some salesmen

Carson Kreitzer

Play
30s-40s
Seriocomic
Contemporary

Jolene Palmer (Jo) is a prostitute on death row for killing seven johns.

Now they got their fucking movie coming out, and I haven't even been convicted yet. That's gotta be illegal. I swear. *First Female Serial Killer.* And I haven't even been' convicted yet. I'm right in the middle of this shit.

An' they got me bein' played by SOMEBODY I NEVER EVEN HEARD OF. They coulda at least got Jodie Foster or something. I know I . . . ain't that pretty, but they could rough her up some. We know she can playa hooker. She was real good in that *Taxi Driver.* Actually, I looked . . . well, I looked a lot like her when that movie came out. Don't look nothing like her now. Maybe I would, if I got to go home after shooting, instead a . . . 'Course, at that time home was a car out in the woods. Fuckin' . . . freezing. I was cold all my life, Florida always sounded like a good deal.

Anyway, we know she can playa hooker, we know she can get raped. How about coming full circle and we see her packin' a little Justice? Huh? Now there's a movie I'd pay money to see.

Not some fuckin' bullshit lying-ass TV crap fuckin' Marg Helgenberger fuckin' Alyssa Milano. Who the fuck are these people?

Serial Monogamy

Alison Bechdel

Illustrated Novel
30s
Comic
Contemporary

A young woman attempts to find peace in being alone—or being with someone—or . . .

I know I'd be better at relationships, if I were only more ACCEPTING, more LAID-BACK, more IN-THE-MOMENT, MORE AT PEACE WITH THE UNIVERSE!! I'm trying! I'm trying!

Maybe the problem is I'm asking too much. MAYBE you can't HAVE both long-term stability and searing passion. Or finely tuned emotional intimacy and compatible living habits. Or highly charged intellectual rapport and a similar taste in music. I know you can't expect one person to meet all your needs . . . but just how many CAN you reasonably expect them to meet? When things get hard in a relationship, how do you know when to keep working on it and when it's futile? Is it quitting if you leave, or giving up if you stay? And what does it mean to TRUST someone?

Compelling questions. But isn't that precisely the essence and glory of the lesbian experience? To question, to strive, to transcend outmoded paradigms of behavior? How fortunate I am to be part of this great experiment. How THRILLING to be free of the SUFFOCATING CONSTRAINTS, the SHACKLES and TRAMMELS of THOUSANDS of YEARS of heterosexual DOGMA and CONVENTION! (. . .)

Still the picket fence would be awful nice . . .

Sexual Perversity in Chicago
David Mamet

Play
20s
Comic
Contemporary

*Joan, a kindergarten teacher, appears to be a young woman
who knows her way around, but she's just as confused about
men and sex as the next woman. She has just caught two of her
kindergartners engaging in some sexual exploration, which
mystifies her further.*

What are you doing? Where are you going? What are you
doing? You stay right there. Now. What were the two of you
doing? I'm just asking a simple question. There's nothing to be
ashamed of. (*Pause.*) I can wait. (*Pause.*) Were you playing
"Doctor"? (*Pause.*) "Doctor." Don't play dumb with me, just
answer the question. You know that attitude is going to get you
in a lot of trouble someday. Were you playing with each other's
genitals? Each other's—"pee-pees?"—whatever you call them at
home, that's what I'm asking. And don't play dumb, because I
saw what you were doing, so just own up to it. (*Pause.*) All
right—no. No, stop that, there's no reason for tears—It's perfectly—natural. But—there's a time and a place for everything.
Now—no, it's all right. Come on. Come on, we're all going in
the other room, and we're going to wash our hands. And then
Miss Webber is going to call our parents.

Silent Heroes

Linda Escalera Baggs

Play
Late 30s-early 40s
Dramatic
Contemporary

Kitty, unsure if her Marine husband is dead or alive, in empathizing with Eleanor, reveals much about herself.

Eleanor's no different from the rest of us. She has to sit through long deployments. With no contact except letters . . . suppose in the middle of a really difficult tour of duty, she slipped. Once. That's all. You wouldn't condemn her for that would you? I mean, you'd be able to understand the loneliness, and the fear, and need to be normal and feel like you can call the shots . . . and, and imagine it's Christmas. And she's visiting her home-town and she runs into her old beau and the squadron just lost three planes—four dead, two POWs, and she didn't think she could take any of it anymore, and she wanted to pretend it didn't matter too much—she wanted to prove she'd be able to survive alone . . . if she had to, I mean . . . And if it only hap-pened once, and she never told anybody and it was just eating away at her and then on nights like tonight, when she thinks he might not come home, and she feels so incredibly awful and . . . you'd understand, wouldn't you?

Small Domestic Acts

Joan Lipkin

Play
40s
Dramatic
Contemporary

Frankie is a butch, working-class lesbian, a doer not a talker. In this scene she has been arguing with her lover, Sheila, who is unhappy about their style of communication. She alternately shifts in her address from the audience to her lover.

Aw, Christ. Why do I have to put it in words? It's just that . . . when I try to . . . couldn't. I don't know why. And the more you want me to, the less I can. You know, it's funny. I have so many conversations in my head but when it's time to open my mouth, the words just leave me. I love Sheila. I love coming home, making love to her, fixing things around the house. But that's not enough. You want more. You want me to talk all the time and I just don't know what to say. (. . .) I don't really think anybody can understand another person, anyway. At least, not the way it is for me. I don't know. See, this is exactly what I don't like. All this deep talk and thinking. It leads nowhere. I get so frustrated. But Sheila. You want words. Spoken *out loud* words. And no matter what else I give you or do for you, it isn't enough. She thinks I'm holding back. Maybe I am. Sometimes, when we're lying in bed at night and I hear the sound of her breathing, I start to choke. I look at her lying there next to me. I see the curve of her breast. This need rises up in me so deep, I can't think where she begins and I leave off. And then when she looks at me with those big eyes, I can't say anything.

Small Domestic Acts

Joan Lipkin

Play
30s-40s
Dramatic
Contemporary

Much to her surprise, Sheila has discovered that she has fallen in love with a woman and now has to make a decision about what she should do.

Just because I'm not in love with him doesn't mean I don't have feelings. *In love.* Whatever that means. That's the thing about talking, isn't it? You talk to be understood and yet the only words I know sometimes make it impossible. I have feelings for Frank. How could I not? We live in the same house. We sleep in the same bed. But lately, I feel like I've been living a half-life, like I'm sleepwalking my way through life. Is it my fault that I woke up? Or started having different dreams? Is that wrong? Life is so short. You've got to make a decision sometimes. But then, when I think about leaving, I get terrified. It's like stepping off a cliff. I don't know who or what is waiting for me on the other side. And will I fly or hit the ground with a sickening thud? *(Beat.)* It's never easy to leave someone if you care for them at all. But is it fair to him or me to stay, feeling like I do?

Small Domestic Acts

Joan Lipkin

Play
30s-40s
Dramatic
Contemporary

Sheila is discovering that she is unsure she wants to remain with Frank, the man with whom she has been living for several years. She reflects on how it is that she came to be with this man.

I was OK on my own. I had a job and a regular bank account. It wasn't much, what with the rent and the utilities and my car payment. It was the first time I had something that was all mine. But damn if my friends didn't make me feel like I was doing something all wrong. There we'd be, having a pizza, or a few drinks, and it would be men. And if they weren't talking about men, they'd be working real hard *not* to talk about them. Laughing too loud, tossing their hair back at the bar. I figured the only way to get away from this man thing . . . was to get one. So when I met Frank and liked him OK, I thought this is it. You've got to make a decision sometimes. So this thing with Frank happened pretty quickly. Before I know it, we're living together. One day, I wake up and say, who is this man I sleep next to every night? Who is he really? Who am I? *(Beat.)* When I think back on how nervous I was. Would he like me? And would it be OK in bed? Shoot, that's the easy part. Talking and getting along day to day is what's hard. All I could think about was would he like me. I was so busy thinking about would he like me, I never stopped to think . . . did I like him?

So This Is It?

Erin Brodersen

Original Monologue
20s+
Dramatic
Contemporary

A young woman empathizes with a dead cat.

The other day during rush hour I drove past a little boy stand-ing on a steep hill, which was presumably his hill, watching as the steady stream of cars, re-ran over a cat, also presumably his cat. He didn't flinch as each car reiterated the fact that his cat was now dead.

I imagine that because it was rush hour he had not been able to run into the road to save his cat from the onslaught of cars streaming past his house. Because he knew not to go running out into the street. That's what separates him from the cat in this story. He knew better.

He had chased it outside yelling "no kitty, no!" then stopped, knowing that his cat was going to be hit and that there was no way to stop it now. It must have been one of those seconds that seem like a minute, because he came to the realization that he can't protect everything.

I am a cat who never knew better, and you are little boys who did, and this is just how things have to end sometimes.

The Speed of Darkness

Steve Tesich

Play
16-18
Dramatic
Contemporary

Mary is a young woman on the verge of leaving home. She has just read aloud a passage by James Agee about "family," and has become emotional.

Oh, Dad, I was such a fool. I was looking forward to it so much. My last year of school. Going off to college. I had no idea it would be like this. (. . .)

It's like waiting to die or something. I've loved it all so much. I had you and Mom, I had lots of friends. I had my favorite teachers. And now it's all ending. The teachers I admired don't sound so smart anymore. I don't know why they don't. I'm sure they're exactly the same as they've always been and I'm the one who's changing. Looking at them differently. I don't want to do that. None of my really good friends are going to college. And they're not my friends anymore. Not like they were. It's like they've all started pulling back. All except Eddie. It's like we've all started saying good-bye in installments. I dread graduation day. I just dread it.

The Speed of Darkness

Steve Tesich

Play
40s
Dramatic
Contemporary

Anne lived out her youth against the backdrop of the sixties: free love and the Vietnam War. Here she tells her veteran husband how strongly she feels about telling their daughter the truth about her birth.

I wish I'd known ahead of time that I'd meet you. I would've lived differently. There'd be nothing now to tell your daughter because she'd be yours, all yours, and I know how a man like you feels about things like that. If she can't be all yours, I can. But this lie is keeping us apart. It's grown as Mary has grown. I almost told her in the car tonight, but I didn't want to do it without you. (. . .)

[JOE: Easy for you to be brave.]

Easy. To tell my daughter that I'd been with so many men that I don't even know who fathered her. To tell her that even when I knew I was carrying her inside of me, I carried on in the same way. God knows what would have happened to us both had I not met you. Don't you see? You weren't the only one saved. You saved both of us. (. . .)

You know I love you, but there's this . . . this feeling: I want to love more. And it feels like the only way we can make room for that love to grow is to get all broken up again and try to mend right. It's like a living child inside of me, this love. It's there and it wants to grow. Don't rob me of it, Joe.

Split Britches

Peggy Shaw, Deborah Margolin, Lois Weaver

Play
Late teens-20s
Dramatic
Contemporary

The Blue Ridge Mountains of Virginia. Cora Jane Gearheart is sweet, complex, shadowy, and not quite right in the head.

[T]hat's the time I was sittin' by the window that's got those little blue bottles on it. I always sit by that window. And I look out and I ask Blanche questions and she tells me. I say Blanche who's that over there and she tells me. And I say what's so-and-so doin' over there and she tells me that. But this one time . . . (. . .) I was lookin' out that window and there was a man lookin' in at me . . . and he was smilin' at me. He wanted to kiss me. Well I didn't want nobody to think nothin' bad about me, Emma, so I went away from that window and I didn't go back.

Until the next day I went back. And he had come there in the night to kiss me. And he wanted people to know he had come there to kiss me because he left his footprints in the snow all the way from the road right up to that window. He wanted to give me a bad reputation. Well I didn't want nobody to think nothin' bad about me, so I put on my coat and I put on Blanche's boots and I went out there and stepped on them footprints . . . all over them footprints . . . a thousand footprints all over his footprints. I didn't want nobody to know he had come there in the night to kiss me. I didn't want nobody to think I had a bad reputation . . .

Storage

Lisa Samra

Original Monologue
20s-30s
Seriocomic
Contemporary

A daughter reports a recent visit home.

ok so i go home to visit my mother for christmas and there are
no christmas decorations up because my brother who lives thirty minutes away and works two minutes away from my mother's doesn't ever come over or offer to do anything for her she's
seventy-one and christmas is very important to her because she
likes it so much plus my father left her alone and went golfing
in arizona the last christmas before he died so i go home and
she says that we're going to take all the christmas stuff and
other stuff down from the crawl space above the linen closet
which is up high which is why she can't do it herself and we're
going to put it in a place in the garage or somewhere where she
can get them herself because obviously my brother is no use to
her in this matter and i agree to do this because i feel very protective of her she being my only living parent and want her to
be happy at christmas time and also because i feel guilty
because when i was a young and irresponsible college student
i took my family christmas tree and all the decorations to my
apartment and then left them in the basement of that apartment
after i moved and so basically i lost the family christmas tree
and all the ornaments some of them very old and dear to her
and she has never let me forget this and even when she doesn't
mention it i feel guilty because her voice is permanently in my
head making me feel stupid and irresponsible but you can't
change the past so i can do all i can now to be there for her
and change her opinion of me

Straight Stitching
Shirley Barrie

Original Monologue
30s
Seriocomic
Contemporary

*Frenchie, a shop steward in a garment factory, advises Mei Lee,
the new worker from Hong Kong, whose sewing machine was
vandalized.*

I tell you a story now, from when I start in this business. I was
the only black in the factory then and they were not nice to me.
Some terrible things were said to me. And my machine too. Oh
yes. I would find the thread gone. Finally I go to my Supervisor
and say—you must do something. This is sabotage. He say to
me—who he gonna blame. And he say—it better for you if you
sort it out for yourself. So I go to the woman who work next to
me and I say, "Listen, good. I going to make your life one big
misery if you don't tell me who is doing these things to my
machine." She told me who it was. So I went to my machine.
And I pick up my screwdriver that I use for fixing my machine.
And I go to the woman who doing these things to my machine.
I lift she up out of her place and I lay she back over the cutting
table. I put the screwdriver to she throat and I say, "You mess
with my machine one time more and this screwdriver ain't coming out dry." And after that, we become good friends.
(*FRENCHIE laughs.*) What the matter, Mei Lee? You got to
learn to stand up for yourself now.

A Streetcar Named Desire

Tennessee Williams

Play
35+
Dramatic
Contemporary

Blanche has lost the family estate to creditors. Here, she defends herself to Stella, her sister.

I, I, *I* took the blows in my face and my body! All of those deaths! The long parade to the graveyard! Father, Mother! Margaret, that dreadful way! So big with it, couldn't be put in a coffin! But had to be burned like rubbish! You just came home in time for the funerals, Stella. And funerals are pretty compared to deaths. Funerals are quiet, but deaths—not always. Sometimes their breathing is hoarse, and sometimes it rattles, and sometimes they even cry out to you, "Don't let me go!" Even the old, sometimes, say, "Don't let me go." As if you were able to stop them! But funerals are quiet, with pretty flowers. And, oh, what gorgeous boxes they pack them away in! Unless you were there at the bed when they cried out, "Hold me!" you'd never suspect there was a struggle for breath and bleeding. You didn't dream, but I saw! Saw! Saw! And now you sit here telling me with your eyes that I let the place go! How in hell do you think all that sickness and dying was paid for? Death is expensive, Miss Stella! (. . .) And I with my pitiful salary at the school. Yes, accuse me! Sit there and stare at me, thinking I let the place go! I let the place go? Where were you! In bed with your—Polack!

Stuck Rubber Baby

Howard Cruse

Novel
45+
Dramatic
Contemporary

Anna Dellyne Pepper is a preacher's wife who, in the early sixties, had been a promising jazz singer. She is speaking to Toland, a young man trying to work through his confusion about his sexual identity.

You've offered to marry Ginger? Well, more power to you. Your folks raised you well. I can't help wonderin', though, if you're lookin' in a clear-eyed way at what the "married life" you're proposin' might turn out to be like.

Somethin' about this is remindin' me of the fix my ol' friend Shelby got in. He was in a band I was with back when I was a singer up North. He was a *good* musician, now! An' Shelby, bless his heart, was as gay as a peacock! (. . .)

But then somethin' made Shelby decide that he just had to go straight. He got married, had children, an' memorized more Bible verses than the Lord Himself ever knew! He built up a whole make-believe world for himself. He walked different, talked different, an' tried to be somebody altogether different from the Shelby we'd known before.

But he couldn't keep up the make-believe, Toland. In time the whole house of cards fell down around him. He wound up with an ex-wife an' three kids who'd lost all respect for him because of his lies. An' the crazy thing was: Everybody respected Shelby when he was gay, but I can't think of a soul who liked him much when he was straight. He wasn't geared toward bein' straight. To put it bluntly, Shelby bein' straight bordered on the ludicrous. Bein' gay, on the other hand, had always come natural to him. Tsk, tsk, tsk! I do miss ol' Shelby!

Oh, not that *you* would be ludicrous playin' straight, sugar! There's not a doubt in my mind you'd pull it off better than Shelby did! Still, I'd think a little more about it if I was you, about tryin' to be what you're not.

the suitors' ward
Clay McLeod Chapman

Short Story
20s
Dramatic
Contemporary

A nurse at a combat hospital finds she has many suitors.

The Red Cross never prepped us nurses for the number of marriage proposals we'd get. (. . .) I'll be on my rounds, when
suddenly one of them will grab me by the wrist and drag me
over to his bed. (. . .)

When I get better, why don't you and me run away?
As soon as I'm on my feet again, let's get hitched.
The second I'm out of this hospital, I'm coming back with a
ring.

The trick is to never say no. You have to keep their hopes up,
so that they'll heal. (. . .) If they won't pull through for themselves, they'll do it for you.

So I started saying yes.

I said yes to Lieutenant Miller, with his torn abdomen.
I said yes to Private Thompson, with three-quarters of his body
covered in third-degree burns.
I said yes to every soldier whose chances at survival continue to
dwindle the more their fear of death overwhelms them. (. . .)

I'm a widow a hundred times over.

This clipboard's my bouquet. It's a floral arrangement of ailments, assorted with a half dozen amputees, sprigs of injuries. I'll toss it to the other nurses once my shift's over, all of them scrambling to grab it—just to see who gets to wed next.

Table of Discontents

Nina Kossman

Play
25-35
Dramatic
Contemporary

Nora, haunted by her loss, confronts her psychiatrist.

I got Baby all ready for the visit to the pediatrician, thinking how pleasantly surprised the good doctor will be to see her walk. When the phone rang, I said to Zef, "Take Baby to the car, I'll be there in a second, I'll just get the phone." It was Varya, my old acquaintance. She would call me every couple of weeks with the same question; and out of a sort of kindness I would give her the same answer. Meanwhile, Zef stormed back in, put Baby down and said that if I don't hurry up I'll have to take Baby to the doctor without his help, that is, without the car. Varya started asking her question, but I said, I can't talk now, Varya, I'm in a rush to get Baby to the doctor. I felt bad hanging up on her, but did I have any choice? That's when I noticed that Zef had left the front door open on his way in, and I said, "Where's Baby?" We went outside, walked up and down our short block. He called, "Baby! Baby!" I fell on my knees and howled like a wounded animal. Neighbors started coming outside, asking each other what happened because they didn't dare ask us. Then the police came, made a written report, searched the streets, returned empty-handed.

I came here, because they say that talking helps. So I paid you to listen to me, and now I'm done, and you can go back to thinking about what to get for dinner.

Taking Sides
Clinton A. Johnson

Original Monologue
20s
Seriocomic
Contemporary

An angry Sister has something to say to thieving white women.

I am tired of white women taking things from me.

Last Wednesday, my boyfriend, Ty comes to tell me that he and "my so-called best friend Stacy" have "developed feelings for each other." I said what about your feelings for me? And he says that's all over. He says he thinks Stacy can take him places that I can't. I told him it sounds like he wants a real estate agent. (. . .)

She saw me Thursday, turns around and runs away all crying and everything. It's a good thing she ran. I would have given Little Miss Ally McBeel something to cry about.

What kind of low, trifling, hair-dye, piece of white trash sticks her skinny little ass in *my* business. He was my man! Truth be told, he wasn't much, but he was mine! Now, it's hard, it is so hard, to find a halfway decent brother to spend time with. On top of that, I've got to worry about some white chick pulling him away every time she catches a little bit of jungle fever! Dammit, I was almost done breaking him in! Now what am I going to do with him once you've used him up and tossed him aside? You're gonna' take what you want, but why do you want him? Can't you at least leave us our men?

Tammy
Rob Matsushita

Radio Play
60+
Comic
Contemporary

Tammy, a grandmother, widens the generation gap.

I don't know if I ever told you this—I wanted to be the lead guitar in a hardcore band.

But, see, these fingers . . .

Yeah.

I mean, now, forget about it, but at fifty-seven, they were still pretty strong.

But your father said no. Didn't want to hear the noise.

He did like our concept, though. All hardcore covers of show tunes. We had an arrangement of "Poor Jud is Dead" that blew the doors down, I tell you!

But, no, he didn't go for it. He withstood it that one session, but that was it. You were away at college at that point.

Who taught me . . . ? Some kid, in the 70s. Tony. Tony Delano. Nice boy. I used to sell him pot.

Oh, that was years ago.

You've never even heard about your father's freebasing period. That was a hoot and a holler, I'll tell you.

Oh, yes, your father was quite the live wire, then. He always used to say to me, "Tammy, you my firecracker!"

And we'd laugh, and laugh, and laugh.

Of course, considering how much pot and crystal meth was floating around, we laughed at a tremendous lot of things.

No, for some reason, you kids never found out about that stuff.

Oh, Paul, your brother, had some suspicions. When we had the drug talk with him, there's an excellent chance your father was high at the time.

So.

How old is my granddaughter, now?

This Wakeful Night

Rosary O'Neill

Play
20s
Dramatic
Contemporary

December, 1882. The Chopin plantation in Cloutierville, Louisiana. Kate Chopin, a writer and dark-haired Irish beauty, speaks to her husband.

(SHE flattens out pages and inserts them in her manuscript.)

Why write when—it . . . offends others. When . . . I see through ripped pages . . . bleeding mosaics of my life—And must face how little you value me. First, I wrote for courage—I needed a place where—I could hold the anxiety—

(Pause.)

Of course you loved me when I was young and flirtatious. But you dislike the mature me. True, I haven't known what I wanted. I've been living in the confusion of others' needs.

(Pause.)

For twelve years, I put aside my writing whenever a child cried. And children cried all the time. I hoped finally to get a writing life started. Late but started. You said you wouldn't restrict me. I wouldn't get caught wherever I was when I got married. But, you've kept me pregnant—I didn't want this many children. Last time, I prayed God would spare the baby but kill the mother. You've kept me moving. Magazine to Coliseum Street to Louisiana Avenue, each time to a more prestigious address— true—with less money. Too much emphasis is placed on longevity as a sign of a good marriage. I have to feel you're heeding my needs. And I need to write.

'Tis Better

Clinton A. Johnston

Original Monologue
20+
Comic
Contemporary

. . . to give than receive.

You don't do that! You don't just give people gifts!

It's not Chanukah. It's not Christmas. It's not my anniversary. It's not Kwanzaa. It's not my birthday. *Then*, you give gifts. Those are "Gift Giving Days"!

Fine, you give me a gift. What am I supposed to do now, huh? Do I get you a gift? Do I get you a gift now just because you got me a gift? Do I get you the same type of gift? What if your gift is more expensive than mine? Does that mean I love you less? How do we keep track? How do we budget? All these worries are spared us, why? Because we are a civilized society! Because we have rules and tradition and ritual to make sure that the *fabric* of our interactions remains strong and sturdy! But that doesn't work for you, does it? No, you're too good for the bonds and ties that keep us together, you with your over-romanticized views of individualism and your warped confusion of nonconformity with sincerity. You, you self-righteous, peevish, anarchistic putz, you would just go your own way and everyone else be damned! Well, I will not have you bring your culture-smashing chaos into our relationship!

Tomboy

Roger Nieboer

Play
60+
Seriocomic
Contemporary

An extraordinary female athlete, Ms. Toni, recalls a particularly rough day on the diamond.

I don't know why, because usually gettin' called names never really bothers me, but for some reason this guy sets me off. (. . .) I get so mad I can barely see the ball when I come up to bat. Coach give me the bunt sign. I bunt a lot because I'm fast, and I lay a perfect slow-roller down the third base line. Very next pitch I get the steal sign, so off I go. My buddy is blockin' the bag at second, so I hook around to the right of the bag and reach in with my left hand. It's close, but I'm safe. I'm laying there face down in the dirt when I feel it. A sharp sting rips right down my back. He just gave me the dirty double knee drop. Square in the kidneys. Now I don't know if you ever been hit there, if you know what it feels like, but if you has, you will never forget. I just lay there moanin' and groanin' til finally the ump calls time. I can't even catch my breath enough to tell any-body what happened. When they ask if I'm OK, I just nod. There's absolutely no way in hell I'm comin' outta this game. I got a job to do. (. . .) Couple innings later, my buddy's up to bat. I'm hopin' he gets on. I know that's wrong, but I'm rootin' and cheerin' deep in my heart for him to get a hit and cross my path. He swats a little blooper into shallow left. It drops an' he tries to stretch it into a double. I reach back with a wild ol' roundhouse and belt him across the beak with all the power I can muster. You can hear the cartilage crack all the way to Corpus Christi. He's squirtin' blood like a stuck pig. He's squealin' like one, too. (. . .) To win a fight, you gotta draw blood. Once you do that, you win. (. . .) I feel kinda bad about it, but what else could I do?

The Trophy Room
Hilly Hicks, Jr.

Play
20s
Dramatic
Contemporary

Lisette describes a moment of double betrayal.

I loved Lewis! I trusted him. *(Beat.)* I loved him so much, when I found out I was gon' be a mother, I wasn't even scared. I was happy. I was smiling and singing to myself. I wasn't worried at all. I went in my bedroom and locked the door. And I sat up in front of the mirror and took off my blouse. Took off my skirt. And I stared at myself, looking for the spot where I was gonna get big. I rubbed my hand over it. And over it. And over it. 'Til I thought I could feel my little baby in there . . . *(Beat.)* I wasn't gon' tell my mama about it. I was just gonna leave and not get her mad. But I wanted Lewis to come with me. I thought we were in love enough to be a family, so I asked him to come with me. *(A pause.)* But he didn't want the baby. He wanted me to give it up. "I wanna live a little more life, Lisette." I told him how happy the baby made me, but he didn't want anything to do with it. 'Cause he wanted to "live a little more life." So I told my mama. I told her I was in trouble . . . And she told me to leave . . .

The Trophy Room

Hilly Hicks, Jr.

Play
20s
Dramatic
Contemporary

Lisette tells Joel about her pregnancy, and the last time she saw Joel's son, the baby's father.

Let me finish. Let me tell y'all the truth. I moved in with my cousin down in Riverside. But she didn't want anybody knowing about me. She said I was bringing shame under her roof. I didn't see anybody. I didn't go anywhere. I didn't do anything. I was just waiting. I was sitting in front of the mirror, watching myself get big. 'Til pretty soon I couldn't watch anymore. After a while, I would just sit down with a blanket and cover myself up so my cousin couldn't see it and I didn't have to look at it. She said as soon as the baby came, I was gon' have to go. But I didn't wait that long. *(Beat.)* I came back to L.A. I might've disappeared, Mr. Porter. But I came back. And Lewis did see me again. He saw me when I was as big as I ever got. I found him smoking a cigarette in the parking lot next to that restaurant he used to work at. I thought with the baby almost here, it'd be different. I wasn't smiling or singing anymore. I was scared to death. I didn't know what he was gonna do. *(Beat.)* When he saw me, he had a look on his face like he didn't remember me. I said, "Why're you looking at me like that, Lewis? This is your baby, too." Then he reached down and felt where the baby was, and he told me . . . he still loved me. He told me it made him sad that I was gone so long. And he wanted to take care of me.

Tumor
Sheila Callaghan

Play
Early 20s
Seriocomic
Contemporary

Sarah has a bad shopping experience.

Walking around the women's department in Macy's. There are
children everywhere, crawling like arachnids, they have more
legs than I thought children were supposed to have but I guess
you start to notice these things when you've been hijacked.
Looking over their sweaty heads for something simple and
angora I recall when angora was simple, when the angora gaze
was not flecked with knots of unfiltered mess who run for no
reason and stick to everything and wail like original sin multi-
plied by twelve.

I keep my eyes a safe distance above the swarming ick and spot
a garment worthy of my onceupon self. I move towards it as
smooth as a rollerball pen. Soon I am close enough to attract its
static cling. My hand, electric, rises to the rising sweater arm,
also electric, and in our dual reaching pose we are an Italian
Renaissance masterpiece. But as my fingers splay for the grasp I
feel an icy sludge make its way down my left leg. I hear this:
"It's not my fault, the bottom fell out!" And then a small person is galloping away from me towards a larger person. I look.
My entire calf from knee to ankle is covered in a seeping red
liquid. Pooling into the side of my sneaker is roughly eight

ounces of bright red smashed ice. And lying next to my foot is a Slurpie cup with its bottom in shreds.

That night I dream of buckets and buckets of blood gushing from between my legs.

Twirler

Jane Martin

Play
Early 20s
Dramatic
Contemporary

A young baton twirler admires a deceased competitor and the spiritual mysteries of their art.

God, Charlene Ann Morrison. God, Charlene Ann! She was inspired by something beyond man. She won the nationals nine years in a row. Unparalleled and unrepeatable. The last two years she had leukemia and at the end you could see through her hands when she twirled. Charlene Ann died with a 'ton thirty feet up, her momma swears on that. I roomed with Charlene at a regional in Fargo, and she may have been fibbin', but she said there was a day when her 'tons erased while they turned. Like the sky was a sheet of rain and the 'tons were car wipers and when she had erased this certain part of the sky you could see the face of the Lord God Jesus, and his hair was all rhinestones and he was doing this incredible singing like the sound of a piccolo. The people who said that Charlene was crazy probably never twirled a day in their life.

Two Rooms
Lee Blessing

Play
30s
Dramatic
Contemporary

Lainie and Michael are American educators in Beirut. Michael has been taken hostage. In this scene, an American reporter is trying to convince Lainie to give interviews and publicize her husband's kidnapping.

Get out of here! (. . .)

(A beat.) You know what will get him back? Nothing we can understand. Whatever took Michael, whatever will bring him back is a power so incomprehensible we'll never understand it. And all the running around screaming about injustice won't change a thing. All we can do—all *anyone* can do—is take pictures of mourning widows. Write stories about mourning widows. Become fascinated with widows of men who aren't even dead yet. But nothing—*nothing*—will make a difference. (. . .)

Get out! If I want to see a scavenger, I'll go to the marsh.

Vanishing Marion

Jeanmarie Williams

Play
17
Comic
Contemporary

Kathleen, a senior in high school, has just come from AP Bio class.

It's not fair.

My brain was perfect. Perfect. You have no idea . . . the time I spent. I measured everything to scale. I rolled the Playdough, I made the . . . meninges, I mean, wafer thin actual meninges, do you have any idea how hard it is to mold Fruit Roll-ups? I mean, crap, I created an actual, real-to-scale, complete with all the glands in the right place, three-pound model of a human brain.

Nancy Simmer! I mean, Nancy Simmer paints a musical note on one side of her pathetic, plaster-of-Paris fourth-grade-social-studies-project brain, and sticks a mathematical formula on the other and then has the nerve to say "Oh, *my* brain is an interpretation. *My* brain is the *essence* of—"

No one told me to interpret anything. No one told me to be abstract. Mrs. Schwartz never said—I did it the right way, and I lose! More than that, I lose *and* I get a B?

She had slides and . . . she dimmed the lights and played Nine Inch Nails! This creative learning crap is way out of control.

Don't they realize that we'll all get to college, and like, Nancy Simmer won't know anything. I mean, so, great, she'll have . . . ideas . . . about things. Big deal, ideas. But she but she won't *know* anything. She won't know *dick* about a brain even though she got an A in AP Bio! It's not fair! It's not fair to me. It's not fair to Nancy. It's not fair to any of us!

What ever happened to getting it right?

Vent
Sean Patrick Doyle

Play
Late 20s
Seriocomic
Contemporary

A very slender young mother tells of a frighteningly obese family, who are concerned about her "anorexia."

They are on a campaign against my metabolism. I mean . . . it's not like I mind the baklava, but when they bring out the tub of macaroni and cheese, screaming, "Let's fatten you up, hun!" . . . my God do the chunks start to rise. I have never seen so much macaroni and cheese in my life. When they scoop it out onto their large plates with little pigs on them . . . it makes a noise. It just makes me cringe. Let me tell you. It is like the magnified sound of a moving snail.

But I don't dread that nearly as much as the parade of little fat children. Downing a whole bottle of Hershey's chocolate syrup. Tommy, their four-year old son, calls me "Anorexa." His mother corrects him by saying "Anorexia, honey . . . but that isn't nice dear." It's the perfect reflection of what they say about me when I step out of the home, passing over the doormat that says, "Live it Large."

And the odd thing is that they get such satisfaction out of when I *do* delve into the Ziplock bag full of cookies. Like they are helping me overcome some health issue. They are taking the kind of credit their doctor will take when he performs a triple bypass surgery on Mrs. Windham. Really.

Viral Soup

Antay Bilgutay

Play
Late 30s
Seriocomic
Contemporary

Gillian is an AIDS nurse. She addresses the audience in response to her friend Todd's breakup with a boyfriend.

I read an article in *The New Yorker* that talked about a woman with HPV. It called her vagina a Crock-Pot of viral soup. I know. I haven't made chili since. Every day, I read about some new disease, some new strain of some old disease. I just want to scream. The real infection, the thing we need to stop, is these people who don't know how to love. They spoil it for the rest of us.

Like these people who hang onto the bitterness of all their old breakups. People, listen to me. *Let. It. Go.* The world changes. We've got e-mail and TiVo. *The New Yorker* publishes letters to the editor. If Tina Brown can move on, so can you.

God, what if we did that with everything that ever let us down? Imagine: You buy a gallon of fresh milk. You skip breakfast a couple of times and that last pint of milk goes bad. *Damn you, milk! You turned on me! Never will I buy milk again.* It doesn't happen that way. We give that next gallon jug a chance. Are people less worthy of our faith than milk? Why would you hold onto your pain, like it has value, like it's a treasure? I'm not being callous; I mean, I get it. To feel that much pain, you must have felt that much love, and we remember the love by its tombstone. But you've got to finish mourning and move on.

Volar

Judith Ortiz Cofer

Essay
30+
Dramatic
Contemporary

A Puerto Rican woman recalls her childhood escape.

At twelve I was an avid consumer of comic books—*Supergirl* being my favorite. (. . .) I had a recurring dream in those days: that I had long blond hair and could fly. In my dream I climbed the stairs to the top of our apartment building as myself, but as I went up each flight, changes would be taking place. Step by step I would fill out; my legs would grow long, my arms harden into steel, and my hair would magically go straight and turn a golden color. Of course I would add the bonus of breasts, but not too large; Supergirl had to be aerodynamic. Sleek and hard as a supersonic missile. Once on the roof, my parents safely asleep in their beds, I would get on tip-toe, arms outstretched in the position for flight and jump out my fifty-story-high window into the black lake of the sky. From up there, over the rooftops, I could see everything, even beyond the few blocks of our barrio; (. . .) In the mornings I'd wake up in my tiny bedroom (. . .) and find myself back in my body: my tight curls still clinging to my head, skinny arms and legs and flat chest unchanged.

In the kitchen, my mother and father would be talking softly over a café con leche. (. . .) I would stay in my bed recalling my dreams of flight, perhaps planning my next flight.

War of the Buttons
Jonathan Dorf

Play
Teen
Dramatic
Contemporary

Trace is talking to Charlie. Nearby are a group of their friends.

I'll stand in front of you so nobody can see.
    (Beat. CHARLIE sits, his back to the others and to the audience.)
    Do you want me to talk, just in case, so nobody'll hear?
    (CHARLIE nods, already starting to shake quietly with sobs.)
    Have you started yet?
    (Beat.)
    Sometimes I feel like I have to cry, and it's like when you have to sneeze—no, more like when you have to go to the bathroom really bad, and you try to hold it—but if you try to hold it too long . . . That happened to Gene once. When we were ten. He didn't go at the rest stop like our dad told him to, and then five minutes later, Gene says he has to go really bad. We try to pull over, but he can't hold it. Then we have to stop at the first rest stop, so Gene can clean up. My dad made Gene clean the car too. Don't tell Gene I told you. Should I keep going?
    (Beat.)
    Let me know if you have to do it again.

Waving Good-bye

Jamie Pachino

Play
17
Dramatic
Contemporary

Lily Blue is a bright, promising photographer, as was her deceased mother.

This was my favorite thing she ever did. I was ten when I saw it the first time. She had gone off to . . . the Serengeti I think. The month of March is supposed to be, I don't know—she has this thing about light and water and—she'd gone off before, but this time we were pretty sure she wasn't coming back. (. . .) So he took me to this locker where she kept her early stuff, because he wanted me to know something about her. To under-stand why she was right, he said, to go away when the world asked her to, because of what the world got back. Not me, not him, just . . . the world. But there aren't so many ways to say that to a ten-year-old, so he took me to see her work. (. . .)

He showed me all the work she'd done right after they met, and told me how she ate Hershey bars at 12,000 feet after climbing without any of the right equipment, and how it was a miracle she didn't die right there. He smiled so big when he explained how those first pieces made her name, how her vision of him had made her—who she turned into—even though she had grown past them and wouldn't look at them anymore. Even though they were his favorites, and my favorites, she had to go off hunting new light. They were so incredible, I almost for-gave her.

We Were the Mulvaneys

Joyce Carol Oates

Novel
50+
Dramatic
Contemporary

*Corinne Mulvaney, speaking to her seventeen-year-old, Judd,
explains away her husband's abusiveness.*

Your father loves you, honey. He loves you all, you know that
don't you? (. . .)

It's just that he loses control sometimes. As soon as he gets the
business established again, and gets back to work, you know
how he loves to work, he'll be fine. The drinking is only tempo-
rary—it's like medicine for him, like he has a terrible headache
and needs to anesthetize himself, you can sympathize with that,
Judd, can't you? We might be the same way in his place. He's a
good, decent man who only wants to provide for his family.
He's told me how sorry he is, and he'd tell you except—well,
you know how he is, how men are. He loves you no matter
what he says or does, you know that don't you? He's been
under so much pressure it's like his head, his skull, is being
squeezed. Once, a long time ago, I read a story about an Italian
worker who has a terrible, tragic accident on a construction
site, a load of wet concrete overturns on him—"Christ in
Concrete" was the title, I think—oh, I never forgot that
story!—it was so real, so terrifying how the poor man was
trapped—in hardening concrete that squeezed him to death,
broke his bones and his skull and there was nothing anyone
could do—

What a Thought

Shirley Jackson

Short Story
30+
Seriocomic
Contemporary

A happily married woman contemplates killing her husband as he reads the paper.

What a terrible thought to have, whatever made me think of such a thing? Probably a perverted affectionate gesture, [*and she laughed.*]

(. . .) it's not that I don't love him, I just feel morbid tonight. As though something bad were going to happen. A telegram coming, or the refrigerator breaking down. (. . .)

Look, (. . .) look, this is perfectly ridiculous. (. . .)

I don't want to kill my husband (. . .) I never dreamed of killing him. I want him to live. Stop it, stop it. (. . .) What would I do without him? [*she wondered*]. How would I live, who would ever marry me, where would I go? What would I do with all the furniture, crying when I saw his picture, burning his old letters. I could give his suits away, but what would I do with the house? Who would take care of the income tax? I love my husband, [*Margaret told herself emphatically;*] I must stop thinking like this. It's like an idiot tune running through my head.

(. . .) They say if you soak a cigarette in water overnight the water will be almost pure nicotine by morning, and deadly poisonous. You can put it in coffee and it won't taste.

Where Men Are Empty Overcoats

Eric R. Pfeffinger

Play
15
Seriocomic
Contemporary

Agatha Angell, no ordinary teen, notices changes in her world since her brother came out.

Funny thing is this. It had started to get around at school. About George. About how he'd come out of the closet. I don't know how, it's like he'd released something into the air or something, and the other kids had picked up on it like meteorologists. After Christmas break, they started coming up to me in the cafeteria, asking about him. Sidling into the desk next to me in class, going "What's up?" Guys started asking me out. Baseball players and stuff. Asking. Me. Out. Very annoying. It's like what I was saying before, this little glimpse of difference is such a welcome change from the unswerving sameness of everyday life. "She's got a gay brother." They thought one of the other kids was gay they'd beat him up, but when it's my brother it's, like, exotic. Sophisticated. Like I'm some kind of ninth-grade Anaïs Nin.

Of course, Mom and Dad aren't big on difference. Same is good, with them. So after the experiment with the Gay-No-More brainwashing clinic in the strip mall crashed and burned, they regrouped. By the time George came home for Easter weekend, they'd decided that being cheerful and supportive—

just like George always thought he wanted them to be—would help to make it feel more normal, more average, less scary. Leave it to my parents to make open and frank acceptance into another kind of denial.

The Winkleigh Murders

Don Nigro

Play
20s
Dramatic
Contemporary

Bronwyn is the heiress of Winkleigh, an English estate. Terrible things have happened there, including the recent death of her dead brother's friend, Cedric, in a supposed hunting accident. His death brought back terrible memories of her father, which she shares with her admirer, Charles.

I often think of Father, beating his horse, riding his tricycle around and around the harmonium after the chambermaid. Father did have some good qualities. A robust, no-nonsense ability to get things done. A clear head to see through a catechism. A dark sense of humor. Dark as the space between stars. He loved art. Well, he had pictures of ducks. He collected animal heads and obscene topiary. I suppose he was actually quite stupid. Do you know how I got the scar on my lip? I was attacked by dogs as a child. Father was drunk and using me as the fox. He laughed a great deal, reaching his big red hands in to pull me out of the mass of slobbering, snarling hounds, held me high in the air, cried, "Do you scream, lassie? Do you scream?" Then kissed me with his big blubbery lips. I can still smell the liquor and calves' brains on his breath. Childhood is such a magical time.

Winner of the National Book Award: A novel of fame, honor, and really bad weather

Jincy Willett

Novel
Late 30s
Dramatic
Contemporary

In a fit of rising pique, Dorcas defends her overweight sister, Abigail, from a group of well-meaning but overstepping friends who have inappropriately intervened when Abigail backslides on her diet.

Guy, do you know what's wrong with you?
Hilda. Do *you* know what's the matter with you?
Tansy! Do you know what your problem is?
I could say a lot of things. The point is, I won't. The point is that I would never ever, even in the shadow of the gallows, look another adult in the eye and tell him what's wrong with him. This is what we do to *children*. We are not *children*. We are grown people. We are fully formed. We are each of us responsible for and to ourselves. We have a social contract. We treat one another with the respect owed to equals. We see one another's faults and *we keep our own counsel*. We do not *presume* to *improve* our *friends*. Decent people do not take such burdens upon themselves. We are supposed to be decent people. We are all, against the evidence of this sorry day, *mature adults*!

A Woman of Wealth

Stephani Maari Booker

Original Monologue
30s-40s
Dramatic
Contemporary

After her bank refuses to cash a personal check, the speaker lashes out.

My funds have passed back and forth between
my hands and yours for years!
And you treat me like a thief!
Like you're Saks Fifth Avenue and I
just walked in your fancy store
the cash and credit in my pocket worth nothing
because you think Black is the color of poor.

Talking at me with the same stanky tone
that I remember
white social workers, white teachers, white experts
talking at my mother.

Now, when you talk at me like that
You have to pay a price.
Give me what's mine—
My pride, my dignity, and my damn money!

(. . .)

You lost a fortune by dissing me.

I'm rich, rich,—
with my ancestors' blood, their feet walking on the land
that mothered us all, that bursts with gold, diamonds, plat-
inum,
the food that feeds us, the water that quenches us, the trees that
give the air we breathe —
I'm heir to that fortune.

(. . .)

I'm rich — too rich for your thin blood.
I'm rich.
I'm rich.

My treasure beats within this chest . . .
(She raises her right fist and thumps it against her heart.)

Women of a Certain Age

John Paul Porter

Play
40-60
Dramatic
Contemporary

Eleanor sits in a church pew.

I don't like being single, Liddy. One never gets invited to dinner parties. Lunch? Yes. Shopping? Certainly. But when evening comes, there is so much one is cut off from. We get shuffled off to some tiny little spot. Every couple we know got invited to Helen's house out on the island and we don't go. It's nearly August and here we are stuck in the City. We don't belong anywhere. The whole parade is going by and we're upstairs at the window, watching. And you know as well as I the door is closing. So I am going to make this work. With Henry.

Liddy . . . help me. Help me with Henry. You know so much more than me. You could give me good advice. They'll be such a race to grab him. So unseemly. I hate to compete, but what else am I going to do?

Every thing you swear you would never do, everything you despise, sooner or later you wind up doing. Forced into being . . . tacky. Throwing myself at a man.

Your Place or Mine

Le Wilhelm

Play
30s
Comic
Contemporary

After meeting hours before, Peggy finds herself in Mitch's apartment.

I feel as if this experience . . . the one between you and me . . . is real déjà vu. No déjà vu isn't really it. What I am trying to say, Mitch, albeit not well (*Laughs.*) . . . excuse me, I always laugh when I say albeit. What I'm trying to say is that I feel like a time traveler. That's how you . . . this . . . you and me . . . that's how it all makes me feel. Not forward, but back . . . back to the past . . . (. . .) this is like ten years ago . . . maybe not quite . . . maybe a few years more. But like that. It all started when you looked at me and you said, "Your place or mine?" Right then. Just went zooming into the past. You have no idea now long it has been since someone has said that to me. I mean anyone of any quality. And anyone that I just met . . . that very day. Oh, there have been a few, but you know the types they've been . . . or you can imagine. (. . .) The types that look like they're uncircumcised and don't bathe regularly. That type. I have friends that find that type sexy . . . but I don't. Just not my bag . . . if you get my drift. You do, don't you?

MONOLOGUES BY AGE

30+

30s

40+

40s–50s

50s+

60+

MONOLOGUES BY TONE

Seriocomic Monologues

MONOLOGUES BY VOICE

RIGHTS AND PERMISSIONS

2.5 Minute Ride. © 2001 by Lisa Kron. Reprinted by permission of Theatre Communications Group, 520 8th Ave., New York, NY 10018-4156, which has published the entire text.

After Math. © 2005 by Jonathan Dorf. Reprinted by permission of the author.

The Air That I Breathe. © 2004 by Theresa Carilli. Reprinted by permission of the author.

Alchemy of Desire/Dead Man's Blues. © 1994, 2000 by Caridad Svich. Reprinted by Permission of William Morris Agency, Inc., 1325 Ave. of the Americas, New York, NY 10019, on behalf of the author.

All Stories Are True (from *The Stories of John Edgar Wideman*). © 1992 by John Edgar Wideman. Reprinted by permission of Random House, Inc., 1745 Broadway, New York, NY 10019.

American Standard. © 2003 by Jonathan Joy. Reprinted by permission of the author.

And by His Hand, Lightning. © 2004 by Amy Unsworth. Reprinted by permission of the author.

And Now a Word from Our Sponsor. © 2002 by Clinton A. Johnston. Reprinted by permission of the author.

And the Winner Is. © 2003 by David-Matthew Barnes. Reprinted by permission of Playscripts, Inc., who have published the entire text in an acting edition and who handle performance rights (see contact information below).

Angry Young Man. © 2004 by Daniel Trujillo. Reprinted by permission of the author.

Anne. © 2003 by Adam Szymkowicz. Reprinted by permission of Pat McLaughlin, Beacon Artists Agency, 208 W. 30th St. #401, New York, NY 10001.

Animal Husbandry. © 1998 by Laura Zigman. Reprinted by permission of The Dial Press/Dell Publishing, A Division of Random House, Inc., 1745 Broadway, New York, NY 10019.

Approximating Mother. © 1992 by Kathleen Tolan. Reprinted by permission of Peregrine Whittlesey, 279 Central Park West, New York, NY 10024. The entire text has been published in an acting edition by Dramatists Play Service, which also handles performance rights (see contact information below).

At Swim, Two Boys. © 2001 by Jamie O'Neill. Reprinted by permission of Simon & Schuster, 1230 Ave. of the Americas, 10th Fl., New York, NY 10020.

At the Salon. © 2004 by Maureen A. Connolly. Reprinted by permission of the author.

Autumn Come Early. © 2004 by William J. Burns. Reprinted by permission of the author.

Baby in the Basement. © 2003 by David-Matthew Barnes. Reprinted by permission of the author.

The Beard of Avon. © 2001 by Amy Freed. Reprinted by permission of the William Morris Agency, Inc., 1325 Ave. of the Americas, New York, NY 10019. The entire text has been published in an acting edition by Samuel French, Inc., which also handles performance rights (see contact information below).

Bee-luther-hatchee. © 2002 by Thomas Gibbons. Reprinted by permission of Playscripts, Inc., which has published the entire text in an acting edition and which handles performance rights (see contact information below).

Big Boy. © 2004 by Theresa M. Carilli. Reprinted by permission of the author.

Big-Butt Girls, Hard-Headed Women. © 1992 by Rhodessa Jones. Reprinted by permission of the author.

Bird Germs. © 2004 by Eric R. Pfeffinger. Reprinted by permission of the author.

The Blacks: A Clown Show, by Jean Genet. © 1960 by Bernard Frechtman. Copyright Renewed 1988 by Anne Golaz Petroff. Reprinted by permission of Grove/Atlantic, Inc., 841 Broadway, New York, NY 10003-4793, which has published the entire text in a trade edition. Performance rights are handled by Samuel French, Inc. (see contact information below).

Blanca (from *Jails, Hospitals & Hip-Hop and Some People*).© 1998 by Danny Hoch. Reprinted by permission of Villard Books, a division of Random House, Inc., 1745 Broadway, New York, NY 10019.

Bookends. © 1997 by Jonathan Dorf. Reprinted by permission of the author.

Broken Eggs. © 1984 by Eduardo Machado. Reprinted by permission of Pat McLaughlin, Beacon Artists Agency, 208 W. 30th St. #401, New York, NY 10001.

Caitlyn. © 2003 by Steve Mitchell. Reprinted by permission of the author.

Carrie (from "Conception"). © 2004 by Steve A. Lyons. Reprinted by permission of the author.

Cat on a Hot Tin Roof, by Tennessee Williams. © 1954, 1955, 1971, 1975 by The University of the South. Reprinted by permission of New Directions Publishing Corp., 80 8th Ave., New York, NY 10011. The entire text has been published in an acting edition by Dramatists Play Service., Inc., which also handles amateur perform-ance rights (see contact information below).

Charming Billy. © 1998 by Alice McDermott. Reprinted by permission of Farrar, Straus and Giroux, LLC, 19 Union Sq. W., New York, NY 10003.

Cheater Catchers. © 2005 Elizabeth L. Farris. Reprinted by permission of the author.

Cher's Fat Lesbian Daughter. © 2000 by Antay Bilgutay. Reprinted by permission of the author.

Circus Schism. © 2004 by Arthur Jolly. Reprinted by permission of the author.

Conditional Commitment. © 2005 by Terese Pampellonne. Reprinted by permission of the author.

Corn, Hogs and Indians. © 2004 by Avanti A. Pradhan. Reprinted by permission of the author.

Crimes of the Heart. © 1981, 1982 by Beth Henley. Reprinted by permission of William Morris Agency, Inc. 1325 Ave. of the Americas, New York, NY 10019. The entire text has been published in an acting edition by Dramatists Play Service (see contact information below), which also handles performance rights.

The Curious Incident of the Dog in the Night-Time. © 2003 by Mark Haddon. Reprinted by permission of Doubleday, a division of Random House, Inc., 1745 Broadway, New York, NY 10019

Currents. © 1989 by Roger Nieboer. Reprinted by permission of the author.

Curse of the Starving Class. © 1976, 2004 by Sam Shepard, from *Seven Plays by Sam Shepard.* Reprinted by permission of Bantam Books, a division of Random House, Inc., 1745 Broadway, New York, NY 10019. The entire text has been published in an acting edition by Dramatists Play Service (see contact information below), which also handles performance rights.

A Day at the Beach. © 2004 by Beth Sager. Reprinted by permission of the author.

Dear Chuck. © 2002 by Jonathan Dorf. Reprinted by permission of Eldridge Publishing, Box 14367, Tallahassee, FL 32317, which has published the entire text in an acting edition and which handles performance rights.

Distance (from *Enormous Changes at the Last Minute*). © 1971, 1974, 1999, 2002 by Grace Paley. Reprinted by permission of Farrar, Straus and Giroux, LLC, 19 Union Sq. W., New York, NY 10003.

Docent. © 2004 by R. T. Smith. Reprinted by permission of the author.

The Doomsday Club. © 2005 by Terese Pampellone. Reprinted by permission of the author.

The Double Inconstancy by Marivaux. © 1999 by Stephen Wadsworth Zinsser. Reprinted by permission of Bret Adams Ltd., 448 W. 44th St., New York, NY 10026. The entire text has been published by Smith and Kraus, Inc., in *Marivaux: Three Plays.*

Drinking and Diving. © 2005 by David Epstein. Reprinted by permission of the author.

Irene Ziegler Aston is an actor and writer in Richmond, Virginia. Her play, *Rules of the Lake,* won the Mary Roberts Rinehart award. Irene narrated the award-winning documentary film, *In the Face of Evil: Ronald Reagan's War in Word and Deed.* She is completing a novel.

John Capecci is a communications consultant and writer based in Minneapolis. He holds a Ph.D. in Performance Studies and has taught communication performance methods for over fifteen years.